By EDWARD FIELD

Poetry

Stand Up, Friend, with Me (1963)
Variety Photoplays (1967)
Eskimo Songs and Stories (1973)
A Full Heart (1977)
Stars in My Eyes (1978)
The Lost, Dancing (1984)
New and Selected Poems (1987)
Counting Myself Lucky: Selected Poems 1963–1992 (1992)
A Frieze for a Temple of Love (1998)

Fiction (under pseud. Bruce Elliot, with Neil Derrick)

The Potency Clinic (1978)
Die PotenzKlinik (1982)
Village (1982)
The Office (1987)

Anthologies

A Geography of Poets (1979)
A New Geography of Poets (1992)
    (with Gerald Locklin and Charles Stetler)

EDWARD FIELD

A
FRIEZE
FOR
A
TEMPLE
OF
LOVE

BLACK SPARROW PRESS ■ SANTA ROSA ■ 1998

ACKNOWLEDGMENTS

Versions of many of these poems have been published in: *Beloit Poetry Journal, Cafe Review, Chiron Review, Das Ist Alles, Charles Bukowski Recollected, Delos, Exquisite Corpse, 5 AM, Michigan Quarterly Review, Nerve Cowboy, The New Republic, Nexus, Pearl, Pivot, Poetry in Motion, Queer Dog, smellfeast, Solo, Strings, Switched-on Gutenberg, Whoreson Dog,* and *Ziegler Boy.* A section of "The Poetry File" was included in *The Dictionary of Literary Biography #105.*

My apologies to any publication not acknowledged. It is entirely due to my sloppy record keeping.

My thanks to Steve Turtell who went over this manuscript and gave me many useful suggestions; to Robert Myers, who encouraged me to "go for the technology," to my guides in the electronic wilderness, Steve Turtell (again), Michael Sheafe, and David Perotta; and to my lifetime inspiration, Neil Derrick.

Black Sparrow Press books are printed on acid-free paper.

LIBRARY OF CONGRESS CATALOGING-IN-PUBLICATION DATA

Field, Edward, 1924–
    A frieze for a temple of love / Edward Field.
        p.   cm.
    ISBN 1-57423-067-0 (paperback)
    ISBN 1-57423-068-9 (cloth trade)
    ISBN 1-57423-069-7 (signed cloth)
    1. Gay men—Poetry.   2. American poetry—20th century—History and criticism.   I. Title.
PS3556.I37F75   1998
811'.54—dc21

98-12242
CIP

CONTENTS

POEMS 1993–1997

A FRIEZE for A TEMPLE of LOVE

Poems
1993–1997

> *"Edward, I suddenly think, How can I write about being poor and Dris in the* Herald Tribune*? It is insane. I scare myself. Do you know, yes you do and you don't, to suddenly put your life in public where all those people can see it? Don't you think I'm crazy?"*
> —Alfred Chester

THE BOOK OF MY LIFE

—after Bziz (Ahmed Senoussi)

Come, my friends,
    and read
the pages of my heart.
It's an open book,
    my heart.
Take a look.
I call it simply
    My Life—The Book.

The language
    is the one you know,
spoken everywhere
    from high to low,
but more often
    by the low.
It's called
    the language
    of the heart.

Here you will read
    of pleasure, yes,
but much more
    of unhappiness,
and more of failure
    than success.
Do you too cry
    my cry?
Do you too feel
    my rage,
when you read
    of injustices

on every page,
of our rulers' greed,
		rich as they already are,
of your suffering,
of one or another
		senseless war?

Like me,
		you may not understand
exactly why
		life should be so,
though we can guess.
But what to do,
		I think you know
as little as I do—
		yet.
We must talk
		about that, my friend.
Do not forget.

But first,
		read this book,
read it to the end,
		and you will see
that every word
		is true.
Every word,
		is written here
for you.

MORNING SERVICE

בָּרוּךְ אַתָּה יְהֹוָה אֱלֹהֵינוּ מֶלֶךְ הָעוֹלָם שֶׁלֹּא
עָשַׂנִי אִשָּׁה:

Blessed art thou, O Lord our God,
King of the universe,
who hast not made me a woman.

Thank you, God, for not making me a woman,
though if you had,
I'd be the biggest whore in town.

And thank you for that Daddy
I cursed for years.
Even if he whipped off his strap in a rage,
he let me survive—just.
That's all you can ask for these days.
With a lot of help,
I managed to do the rest, though I nearly didn't.
It was touch and go for years.

And while I'm at it, thank God
for my good looks that I despised.
No more. At my age,
you're glad for any advantage.
If I hated my curly hair,
it fell out,
and I'm not sure I regret it.
I can't quite say, Thank God for that.
And since you made me a Jew and nose-crazy,
thank you for the small, straight nose,
though I've never been quite convinced it was.

And thank you for a name
that is not obviously Jewish,
even if it's not me,
or rather I have to thank my father
for changing it.
Name and nose allowed me to stay invisible
when I needed to be, when I couldn't have dealt
with one more problem.

And thank you, God,
for not making me any darker than I am,
though being dark as I was
made me practically an Untouchable
in my WASP town.
But thank God I don't have to cope
with what the Colored cope with every day.
It's a miracle it doesn't drive them all crazy,
but somehow they remain
the salt of the earth.

Thank you, God, for this period
of tolerance in America,
but I don't count on it:
They've gone after us before
and can do it again.

And come to think of it, thank you, God,
for not making me a Russian.
They had free medical, schooling,
full employment, everything,
and look what they have now.
It's true the economy was a mess,
but the principle was right—
all they had to do was make it work.
They even had a great leader
and settled for a jerk.

And how lucky to have seen Andalusia,

Morocco, Tunisia, Afghanistan,
the wonders of the Moslem world.
But thank you, God, thank you,
for not making me
Croat, Serb, or Macedonian—
they're all crazy.
What dopes, they destroyed
their cities, their lives,
and for what?

Thank God the war is far off in the Balkans
and a couple of dozen other places,
but that doesn't mean it's not coming here.
This country too
will fall apart someday,
as the crazies, the insurrectionary armies,
swoop down from the hills,
or our own fundamentalist loonies
find a way of taking over the government.
So thank God for this moment,
even with the horrors beyond the borders,
and watching with dread
what people here are becoming.

And thank you, God, for giving me
somewhere to live, when you could as easily
have dumped me out there
where it's cold and mean,
though of course all gifts are provisional
and I could be in the street tomorrow,
just as any minute we could not be
the richest country in the world,
but flat broke.
And thank you, God, for my dear one,
who is so much trouble
I really have no time
to worry about myself.

COLOMBIAN JOKE

with thanks to Jaime Manrique

1

On the day God
created the earth,
all the angels
flew round and round,
singing chorales
of praise.

But over one place
they stopped,
beating the air
with their angel wings,
as their inspired voices
rose to heaven.
Here alone, they trilled,
*is paradise on earth
and it's called
Colombia!*

Yes, God said,
beaming at them
wickedly,
*but wait till tomorrow
and see
who I'm going
to populate it with.*

2

On the day
God created the planet,
all the angels
flew round and round, singing
chorales of praise.

Day after day they celebrated
as God produced from his fingertips
plants and creatures,
and, according to an ancient tradition,
in a final burst of genius,
a diadem of cities.

A chorus of hallelujahs
rose from the angels
over the glitter
of Paris, London, Rome,
until fluttering in convoy
over Columbia, District of,
they looked down in awe
at God's masterpiece,
a perfect gem of a city
with domed capitol, and avenues
radiating like the rays
around the crown of Athena,
Goddess of Wisdom.

Hail to the city of Washington,
the angels sang,
from whose marble temples
and pillared halls
the people will be justly governed,
and an eternity of goodness
reign over the earth.

Don't be too sure, said God
with his slyest grin.
Wait till tomorrow
and see who I populate it with.

And then I'm going to
do nothing for the rest of time
but sit back and laugh,
watching what happens.

THE JOY OF COOKING

"My most important Household God is food."
—The Dream of Intelligence, *by Sebastian Barker*

1

Men don't generally learn it from their mothers,
and since I knew I was never going to get a wife,
I had to learn to cook for myself.
Of course, I didn't start from scratch.
I remembered things Ma did in the kitchen
and tried to duplicate her dishes,
the few that were any good,
or make them taste the way they should.

She had little culinary talent,
and railed against woman's fate
of slavery to a kitchen stove,
as she popped forth babies spaced out with abortions.
"What about contraception, Ma?" I once asked her,
trying to be grown up.
"Oh, what do you know about it," she snapped back,
as if sex was something that just happened
in the odorous sag of the marital bed.

That same careless attitude she had toward cooking,
and it, too, just happened,
as she tossed ingredients into a pot,
or mixed up a cake that always fell.
By her, it was a sin to follow a recipe.

After she got over an early belief in raw carrots,
which had conveniently simplified her kitchen routine,
her meals were based on the economics

of feeding a large family in the Depression—
lung stew for example, that I couldn't eat now
without a gun to my head or a barf bag handy.
"Good for you,"
which was her whole arsenal of cajolements,
has little to do with the pleasures of eating,
though it is a guiding principle of the culinary art.
All those years, I suffered with a nervous stomach,
as she piled my plate higher and higher
"to fatten me up," she said.
Though this is not about my Oedipus Complex,
I must confess that I wouldn't have minded
murdering my father,
but God, imagine marrying her.

My momma never done tol' me,
but the secret of learning to cook
is a good eater to cook for,
and I connected with one, a terrific guy
who lives more for my cooking
than my bedroom eyes,
but at my age, you know,
a be gezint, or in English,
the important thing is we're happy,
which my analyst would say was impossible.
But besides an obsession with the female breast,
and castration, a word they used
like a *mohel* uses his knife,
the analyst never had anything to say
about the Feeding Syndrome,
an instinct that binds
you, the feeder, to the eater,
as much as it binds the eater to you.
Freud's is too simple a paradigm
if you've married your mother
in the desired shape of a man.
And in any case, my need is to feed him,

however I'm fed.
Which makes me The Mother
in the shape of a man.

2

But men don't have time to stand over a hot stove,
so I don't cook anything that takes
longer than an hour to prepare,
but with basil,
        garlic,
          soy sauce,
            ginger,
               a *ristra* of peppers,
brought back from New Mexico,
                  and a lifetime supply of saffron,
scored on a trip to Morocco and smuggled through customs,
I am out to make everything taste sensationally good,
even with the ingredients available in New York.
When I wander the aisles in the supermarket,
there's practically nothing to buy—
not after shopping in England, France, and Germany,
all over the Mediterranean,
but particularly in the Arab world,
where the brief green explosion of the rainy season
and jewel-like oases in the desert produce,
as Jesus Christ, who came from there, demonstrated,
miracles of food to feed the multitude,
and for pennies.

Though we're raised to be fed,
like Jesus, men are uncomplicated about feeding others,
because, unlike women, we aren't forced into it,
though like Jesus we tend to get involved
in loaves and fishes, or in other words,
food production, mass feeding projects.
And I'm just enough of an old-fashioned lefty

with the maternal instincts of a giant breast
and not a bad cock, either,
to be concerned not to feed only my dear one,
but all the hungry of the world.
The greatest disappointment of my life
was learning that
poetry won't do it.

3

I'm talking home cooking, of course,
so I must register my grouchy minority complaint
against Restaurant Syndrome, the incurable disease
that half of New York is afflicted by
and all my friends, who discuss restaurants
with the same dedication they give
to comparing Callas performances.
When I eat out, I invariably suffer
half the night, swearing Never Again,
and promise myself a whole day of nothing but oatmeal
which I am convinced is the remedy
for all gastric problems, including the fashionable
hiatus hernia, renamed from the lowly heartburn.
The trouble with oatmeal is that I drop weight
faster than a monkey drops his dick when you show him a
        banana
(proving food is more basic than sex?).

But eating for me will always be problematic,
and though I've outgrown my nervous stomach,
I still tend to worry about food, see in it
The Solution to all my problems, and The Problem.
As Reichians once proclaimed the cosmic orgasm
the cure-all, as a Jew I make a religion of food,
even without the thousand and one rituals,
though like an old Jew I often automatically say,
Thank you, Lord—be it for
a meal, an orgasm, or a good shit.

I have a religious belief in corn, for example,
as a gift of the gods.
And lately, I've taken one step downward on the food chain:
I no longer eat calves,
no more than I could knowingly eat dog or cat.
But I will never be a vegetarian,
though I dearly love all the creatures and plants I eat,
and read labels for dangerous additives and refinements.
I mostly lack the paranoia of health nuts
who attempt to achieve perfection by diet,
yet I once went on a green soup purification diet—
three days of it and I looked like a concentration camp victim.
I'm like the fatty who said,
to keep my weight up I have to eat a lot.
And I have to keep repeating to myself
the motto of the terminally skinny:
I HAVE A RIGHT TO EAT.

But never again in restaurants,
except dishes I can't make myself, or won't,
like soft-shelled crabs once a year,
since I can never bear to fry the darlings
alive in hot oil.
I can't help thinking, as I sit there
with friends in restaurants, hating the food
but putting on an act of liking it,
Who can be happy spending
all that money for one meal
when half the world's starving?
Or even, Who can be happy
when half the world is starving?
Actually, I suffer over that,
but for suffering, as for hunger,
eating is the one consolation.

MY SISTER, THE QUEEN

Walking the broad allée past Kensington Palace,
more like a country house, really, than a palace,
where a young Queen Victoria
presides gracefully in stone over royal lawns
sweeping down to the distant mockery
of Henry Moore's giant marble thighbones,

I half-expect to see at an upper window
a familiar figure looking out,
the once-pretty face tear- and mascara-stained,
whisky glass in hand, chain-smoking the cigarettes
forbidden her since the operation.

For a modern Queen, there are more ways than one
to keep a prettier, wilder sister under control
besides locking her in the Tower,
and this one did not hesitate to use her power
to prevent her from marrying
a divorced man, and a commoner to boot,
forcing on her, instead, a loveless marriage
that ended, like a slap in the royal face,
in divorce.

This may be the time, though, when threats
no longer silence her, and I imagine I see
the wretched Princess at the window,
her glass empty and with nothing more to lose,
throwing open the sash and screaming to the world
how her sister has ruined her life.
But just as she is about to hurl herself out,
experienced hands grab her from behind
to clamp over the twisted, hysterical mouth,
and drag her, struggling like a wounded moth,

back inside, where the doctor
waits with the hypodermic,

and as the window slams shut again,
and the heavy drapes, embroidered by the hands
of her sister, the Queen, are drawn,
I blink away the vision
and continue my walk
through the unearthly gardens.

VALLEJO IN PARIS

after "El acento me pende del zapato"
by César Vallejo

Among the French
my Spanish accent dangles
like an extension on my cock.
Bigger than life, it glows through my pants,
magnetic, obscene.
Everybody turns away in horror.
But I know they see it anyway
through the back of their heads.

This is the cruelest answer to my prayers,
glorious but humiliating.
Its size annihilates me here.

When I enter a *urinoir* to take a leak,
a girl passing by catches sight of my huge dong.
I lift my shoulders with a gallic shrug.
What can I do? I'm just a dirty foreigner here.
Nobody will even stand next to me to piss.
So they'd like me to get lost? Why should I care.
I let go my golden shower.

But keep calm, baby, keep calm,
you know secretly everybody's hot for you,
and sure enough, later that night
my phone rings and rings.
It's like the whole city wants a date.

It's my foreign accent that marks me out,
makes me irresistible.

COME BACK, MISS MOFFO, WE LOVE YOU

I don't blame you for only singing in Europe,
the way the *Times'* critic slams you
every time you sing here.
Far better over there where they love you
for your mature voice,
the deep-breasted tones of a woman,
who never minded baring her tits and ass—
in fact, who did it proudly.

Queen of Operetta,
if not Grand Opera anymore,
you are still to most sopranos
what the vaginal orgasm is
to the clitoral.
Where others sound as if they are
having their clits tickled
as they trill through tricky arias,
your voice burbles up thrillingly
from deep inside your vagina,
moist,
rich,
and odorous.

Your childhood near Scranton
couldn't have been much fun,
as the dark little hairy girl in the class
with overdeveloped breasts for her age
and the curse of an operatic voice.
How well I know.
In my town I was the puny dark boy
who carried to school a cello big as me.
I can see you standing up in the assembly
to sing "Ciribiribin,"

while the tough kids
jacked off in the back row, grinning.

Where I grew up, Italians were only slightly
less despised than Jews.
But to be anything ethnic
was humiliating.
And the kids would have crucified you,
as they did anyone
who wasn't the standard product,
especially girls with big boobs.
They had to be sluts.

When you sing those full-breasted tones
with such deep vaginal richness,
it's hard to believe you came from
a town like mine,
but by a miracle escaped
to be transformed gloriously
into yourself.

ANNA MOFFO,
WE LOVE YOU.

FRENCH LESSON: HOTEL D'EUROPE

Cheap Paris hotel, a true bargain,
plus the miracle of firm mattresses.
Madame *la Patronne* attractive, fortyish,
but after ten years, fed up
with running a hotel.
Says she's leaving for L.A. next month
pour les vacances,
hoping to marry there *un industriel,*
who, she says, has *beaucoup de voitures,* many cars.
But when I ask if she speaks English,
she says she'll learn when she gets there.
Something about her blithe confidence
worries me.

She calls me *un homme sérieux,*
which means, I think, that I take
my responsibilities seriously and pay the rent.
I feel flattered that my maturity is recognized.
It is far more substantial
to be *un homme sérieux*
than being simply mature, *un homme mur,*
though I don't have a bean, much less a *voiture.*
The French always make a man of my age
feel *fantastique,*
especially if you look halfway okay.
I hope the industrialist,
surely in her eyes *un homme sérieux*
is serious about marrying her.

Madame *la Patronne* kisses everybody,
especially the handsome tour bus driver,
who arrives, the day we are leaving,
with a busload of German tourists,

They fill the breakfast room on our last morning,
as Madame presides,
helping the clumsiest among us
by breaking open our hunks of *baguette*
and buttering them for us.
Then, baggage in the hall,
we have an affectionate
leave-taking with more kisses.

Even with *beaucoup de voitures*
I somehow don't think *La Patronne*,
handsome as she still is,
will find life in Los Angeles
quite as satisfactory as this.

THE SAFETY

I knew it couldn't last, the Safety—
the years with enough money, a place to live,
and no worry about the police.
But I never forgot
what it was like
out there—
beyond the island of Safety.

I carried around for years
the half-remembered lines
like a prophecy:
"*Doom is dark and deeper*
than any sea-dingle,
upon what man it fall
that he should leave his house…,"

walking in the cold drizzle,
unable to return home,
no friend to go to, no neighbor to trust,
the railroad station a minefield,
the border a trap.
Even sewing a gold coin into my jacket lining
wouldn't help much
when the Safety came to an end.

I never knew how it would end, exactly,
I only knew it would.
It seemed inevitable,
for the bullies never give up.
They only bide their time.

I sometimes wondered, though,
if the safety of death

would rescue me in time....

Though I never believed in it, really,
I clung to the Safety like a baby blanket.
My dreams never reflected the peacefulness,
the orderliness, the ordinariness
of my life.
In the world of dreams
I was always fleeing, as if searching
for a country to live in.
I kept missing trains, planes, and buses,
and often walked around naked, exposed,
where the rest of the world was safely dressed.

The Safety had gone on so long that even Jews
got used to being considered as white people
and considered themselves white,
long enough
for many to forget
what it once was like,
to forget what would surely happen again.

But my kind remembered,
never believed in this normality,
and I was almost relieved when it ended.
The Safety had never felt natural.

And when the thugs moved in again
with their fists and clubs,
I went down under them
almost with relief.

MAGIC WORDS

from the Inuit

In the very earliest times,
when both people and animals
lived on earth,
a PERSON could become
an ANIMAL
if he wanted to
and an ANIMAL
could become a HUMAN BEING.

Sometimes we were
PEOPLE
and sometimes
ANIMALS
and there was no difference—
all spoke the same,
the UNIVERSAL TONGUE.

That was a time
when WORDS were like
MAGIC.
The mind had
MYSTERIOUS POWERS,
and a word uttered by chance
might have
CONSEQUENCES.

It would suddenly
COME ALIVE
and what people wanted to happen
COULD HAPPEN—
all you had to do was

SAY IT.

Nobody could explain it.
That's just the way
it was.

It's one of those old things
that has been
forgotten,
LOST
the way a pebble
drops
from the hand of a child.

How can we find it again
to make things happen
that we want to happen,

HEAL the sick,
FEED the hungry,
HOUSE the homeless,
and HELP
the suffering?

How to find
the syllables
buried deep within us,
the MAGIC WORDS,

TO LIVE

IN PEACE

WITH THE ANIMALS

AGAIN?

HOW TO SPEAK DUTCH

It's helpful to work up a mouthful of spit
in dealing with the three gutturals:
"g" and "r" and "ch" (as in "Bach"),
all gargled, but each different.
It's a heavy workout
like clearing an oyster from your throat.

When a word has s-c-h in it, "*schoen*," (yes, shoe),
you first say the "s," plus "ch" (like in Bach)—
it takes a lot of practice.
Then try "s," "ch," followed by an "r," as in "*s-ch-rijver*,"
and I'm not even mentioning those weird vowels
and dipthongs all their own.
No one not born Dutch will ever get right "*meeuw*,"
the word for seagull.

A woman speaking Dutch must probably
settle for looking wholesome, even earthy,
rather than elegant.
She is forced to work so hard with her whole mouth
and all her teeth
just to get around the words,
it resembles the juicy mastication
of the national treasure, the cow.
In fact, the women are cowlike creatures
popping forth the prettiest boys and girls in the world,
whose rosy innocence makes you long
to ravish the sex of your choice.

The vocabulary is mostly German,
but a more informal variety,
a low German closer to Yiddish,
so no wonder they understand the Jews.

Remember, these are the people the Huns pushed
into the marshes by the sea.
The Dutch are not forgetting that.
They had to work their asses off
making them fit to live in.
But when the Germans need a host for a TV show,
someone to loosen up the audience,
they always get a Dutchman,
because the Dutch radiate good nature,
revelling in the jovial atmosphere they call "*gezellig*"
with its two impossible guttural "g"s.

But above all, the Dutch love the vowel "a,"
pronounced "a-a-ah," and if you frequently say
Oh, ya-a-ah! with a relaxed sigh,
before launching into the story of your day,
that is a good way
to begin to speak Dutch.

MAGICAL MOVIE MOMENTS: "BAHAMAS"

At the subway entrance on Forty-Second Street,
we caught each others' eye, and stopped.
I was eighteen, an office boy,
he was older, broad-shouldered and fair-haired,
and in a courteous southern way he invited me to a movie.
It was after work and I was ready for anything.

Walking toward Times Square together,
he explained his slight limp
by a football injury at a southern university.
I figured he must be in New York
for medical treatment.

He took me to the Paramount Theater,
where the marquee read "Bahamas"
starring Madeleine Carroll and Sterling Hayden.
He paid for my ticket,
but from his clothes and manner
I knew he could easily afford it.

The movie had just opened, and the review in the *Times*
said it was thin on plot.
But with two beautiful blond animals
frolicking half-naked across Caribbean sands
fringed with palms—all in technicolor—
it needed little plot.
We leaned against each other in the darkness
of the back row of the orchestra,
leg pressed to leg,
and as the music swelled
for the glossy lovers on the screen,
we held each others' stiff pricks

under his luxurious coat across our laps,
and brought each other off
for a happy ending.

KILLJOY

When my mother and father
got married
they decided to move
as far away as possible
from the grim slums of the Lower East Side
where they'd been brought
by their parents
from Russia.

So they moved
to Coney Island
at the end of the subway line
by the sea.
But after a while, that too was not far enough,
and they moved again,
this time to the country,
out on Long Island.

It was my father's triumph,
buying a house,
escaping his background and becoming American.
He revelled in the fresh air
when he came home after work.

But my mother hated it,
isolated in WASP America,
and stuck with all those children.
We suffered also,
among people who despised us,
the dark immigrants from the city.
My father didn't want to hear
anything about it.

When the kids on the block yelled
"Christ killer" and "dirty Jew,"
he used to say to us,
"Sticks and stones will break your bones,
but words will never hurt you."

He was partly right:
Words hurt less
than his hard hands, belt, or razor strop,
and are easier to forget.

The flesh remembers
everything.

&

I thought he was just a prude
determined to stamp out
every trace of our sexuality.
My brothers and sisters knew him better.
And his own mother questioned
his going nights to sketch class:
"Ketching, who is he ketching?"
she warned my mother.

My sisters say he was even after
my cousin Ruthie who lived with us,
and their girlfriend Gilda.

And he was peculiar about my sister
who was the star of the art class,
taking her out of high school
after she won the scholarship to Pratt.
"If you want to be an artist," he said,
"stay home and draw."
Then he never let her go out
to show her samples.

40

This was the man who checked at night
to make sure our hands were outside the covers.
When I had my hands in my pockets
he asked, "What have you got in there?"
And I knew the answer had better be, "Nothing."

It was as if his goal was
to make us feel bad about sex.
Our mother spanked us when we played Dirty Stuff
with the other kids on the block
out back under the sumac bushes.
But it never hurt like his hard hand
cracking across your face.

My sisters had engraved on his headstone:

>   LOUIS FIELD
>   ARTIST

I always feel like grabbing a chisel
and correcting it to:

>   ARTIST
>   &
>   KILLJOY

ON HIS POSTURE

someone

who

has published

a book

called

Stand Up, Friend, With Me

had better

not

go

around

slumping

OPERA QUEENS

A composer I know, a neighbor,
once dropped the electrifying news
that the great Anna Moffo has sung his songs,
and telephones him every New Year's.

Whenever I see him on the street,
scurrying along with music scores
clutched to his chest,
I stop him to ask
if Miss Moffo, as I like to call her
in my adoration,
has called him yet
to wish him a Happy New Year.

But he invariably
dismisses my ultimate goddess
with a flick of the hand,
and switches the subject
to Zinka Milanov—
he accompanied Milanov on the piano
during the years of her retirement
as she coached divas with their vocal problems.
"They all came to her,"
he says, in utter worship,
"and Madame Milanov
told everyone the truth.
When Anna,"—
my Miss Moffo is merely "Anna" to him,
in distinction to Milanov,
who is always *Madame* Milanov—
"When Anna came to her
for coaching,
Madame Milanov asked,"—

here the composer's voice purrs slyly—
" 'How old are you, my dear?'
'Fifty-four,' Anna answered.
'My dear,' the composer's eyes
search poor Miss Moffo's neck
for wrinkles, her face for evidence
of a face lift,
'we must be truthful
with each other,
or I cannot help you.
Sixty-four?' "
He cackles in triumph,
as Milanov must have cackled
every time she repeated the story,
and goes on to say
that the last time Anna called him
she said she was working on *Norma*.
"*Norma!*"
He howls with laughter
at the thought.
My tattered queen....

His latest story
is of Renata Scotto
arriving to ask Madame Milanov for help
in singing the dramatic role, *La Gioconda*.
"You want to sing *La Gioconda*?"
purred Madame Milanov.
"Yes," said the reigning diva of the Met,
"it suits my voice."
"My dear," said Madame Milanov,
"Cats are cats
and dogs are dogs,
and *you*
will
never
sing
Gioconda!"

44

And with a dismissive wave of the hand,
he sails down the street
gasping
with Milanovian mirth.

THE MAGIC MOUNTAIN

Instead of the flatland of my youth,
it would have been nice to grow up in a place
with houses on different levels,
and outcroppings of rock.

But best of all would have been a mountain
rising behind the town.
I would have been in love with that mountain
and never stopped climbing it.

I'd get to know the animals and birds
that lived there,
the teeming insect colonies under rotting logs—
I'd learn everything about the mountain.

I'd escape my family
and camp out there overnight,
drink from streams and pee into ferns.
If there was a mountain they couldn't stop me.

There'd be a lot of jacking off on the mountain.
I'd find secret places, caves and grassy hollows,
or in the open, stretched out naked
on warm boulders.

And in an abandoned cabin
with a pile of shit in the corner and smeared paper,
rotted underwear, a used rubber—
I'd jerk off there too.

Sometimes, even, another kid
might be allowed by his mother
to spend the night with me,

and we'd jerk off together in the woods.

Or an abandoned dog would adopt me,
with much leaping about.
I'd jerk him off too,
while he licked my face.

But most wondrous of all, a stranger
hiking through with a hard-on.
I'd go back to that place again and again
and wait for him.

COLOSSUS

It's awesome to have straddled a century,
lived through the peak years of an empire,
that brief period
of absolute supremacy, unlimited wealth,
then the decline and, inescapably,
the fall,
which now looks sooner rather than later.
My country, perhaps we'll crash down together,
and it will be up to archeologists
of some unimaginable future
to figure out how the chunks fit
and which belong to me or it.

It's the classical pattern:
Victory in war brought such power
we could have created a golden age on earth,
had wise men ruled,
but, predictably,
our riches were never used wisely.
As if hungry, we just became
a devouring monster.
In the wrong hands, everything,
the gifts of the gods,
was wasted.

Corrupt and paranoid,
our rulers created a world
of two blocs locked in struggle,
Good versus Evil.
In the name of freedom, we assassinated,
here and abroad, the very people
who might have done the world some good,
and destroyed everything we couldn't control—

other opinions, simple debate, difference,
and were also clever enough
to debase the popular mind
as well as intellectual thought,
by branding generosity of spirit subversive.

That was the dogma we lived by,
so when the other side collapsed,
ours, wealth squandered, corrupt,
was left with a dubious victory.

Awesome to have lived through this drama,
the rise and fall of an empire,
and now, with ignorance more entrenched than ever
and threatening to unleash
final suicidal destruction on the planet,
I, still shakily astride my century, wait
to crumble into ruins with it.

THE TROUBLE WITH STRANGERS

Sex, back then, when I was the whore of Babylon,
what did sex have to do with it?
Sex was really—I see, now that it's practically over—
about other things.
That usually means trouble.

My sex-life had more to do with my need
for attention and flattery, distraction even,
but mostly it was longing to be wanted:
Take me home with you, I was saying.
Please.

My needs could only be satisfied, alas,
temporarily, since the somebody
was always the wrong body, or if the right,
only right for the moment, before
disillusionment, if not disgust, set in—
that's the trouble with strangers.
Anyway, whoever wanted me
had to be wrong.

With what devotion I pursued my needs, almost
to the exclusion of everything else.
It was exhausting. Sex
is not that hard to come by, especially
for a good-looking kid, in a world
teeming with gonad-driven males
needing to come off every day of their lives.
Not that looks have much to do with it,
and more often get in the way of real sex.
What that was I never guessed.
I think it's a special talent,
and if you are without it

you might as well put your energies into work—
something I wanted desperately to do,
except that my desperation drove me
out, day and night.

But my generation, following Freud,
insisted on sex
as life's one solution,
entangling us in a magic jungle
it was almost impossible to escape from.
Only, escaping at the last —
how, I'll never quite figure out—
was my salvation,
since in the jungle, if you do not feed,
you are devoured.

ST. PETERSBURG, 1918

In memory of the USSR

You were sitting on a grassy hummock
in the river as the children
played around you. The water
was flowing lazily.
It was spring,
a perfect day.
I hardly knew who you were,
my mother or what,
it didn't matter.

Across, on the other bank,
young athletes leapt from heights,
lithe in the air,
practicing for the games.
You said you wanted to burn all our money.
I knew it was not so much from idealism
as despair, and I held you
and asked you not to.

It was before everything that happened.
The purges were still to come.
How we believed in the revolution!
That was our youth.
Foolish tears run down my face.
My house of love
would never be so full.

THE BUKOWSKI OPTION

in memoriam Charles Bukowski

An old guy has two choices:
        the Bukowski Option,
which allows you to express all your nastier impulses
        and tell the world to go fuck itself—
this is the Way of Purity, the Bohemian Ideal,
        with its vow never to Sell Out.
On the other hand, whether you sell out or don't,
        you can try, in your old age,
for the discipline of Dignity,
        which is made more difficult
        when you have to take a leak
and every restaurant has a sign in the window,
        "Toilet for customers only."

I lived most of my life as a freak
        which expressed my contempt
        for the capitalist system.
Eventually, though, I too opted for Dignity
        as a protection and disguise
for my battered dreams—
        ideals I still believe in.

But, I ask myself,
        don't you want to be a rebel anymore,
        an example to youth?
Yes, but I'm too dismayed
        by that sagging face in the mirror
and too conceited
        to look like I have dirty underwear
or droopy pants like a full diaper.
        Even Buk didn't grow a beard,

which would at least have saved his five
           most wasted minutes of the day, shaving,
and even have covered the scars
           of acne, drink, and time.
But his beauty was
           that he insisted on thrusting
his entire ugly face in our faces,
           which was tremendously entertaining, of course,
and he knew it,
           even as he snarled at the world.

Can you take the Bukowski Option, I wonder,
           and not turn into a wreck?
What would it be like, I wonder,
           to live like a slob,
and smoke my head off, drink,
           and eat junk food?
I'm too much of a hypochondriac.
           But at some point, maybe,
when there's nothing left to lose?
           As my mother always said,
When you need a drink, you need a drink.
           That time, at least, has come—
frequently.

The Dignified Option would seem to mean
           staying out of sight,
maybe retiring to the country,
           except it's too boring,
especially with the old back
           ruling out gardening.
A composer I knew, like the man without a face,
           would only go out at night
to take long bus rides
           through deserted neighborhoods.
What the hell was he supposed to do?
           Dignity is a good way

54

of disappearing, then even in public
        no one will notice you.
They're all just thankful the old wreck
        isn't being a troublemaker.

But even as a Dignified Gent, it's a constant
        struggle not to be nasty,
because you don't have to be Bukowski
        to have a ball of hatred and disgust
in your gut for the world.
        Though unlike him I'll admit
I'm a sucker for lovey-dovey people.
        Still, I wonder about the pixyish codgers
with their wispy hair and illumined eyes,
        playing giggling Chinese sages
as if old age was a barrel of laughs.
        They've either found something I haven't,
or are frauds.
        I'd guess the latter.

I cringe when I think of that librarian, once,
        cooing at my shrunken, ancient father
and him twinkling back, playing her game. Pitiful!
        Nasty would be better,
like dropping a loud fart, for example,
        in the hush of the library.
The woman at the supermarket checkout counter
        who automatically makes two bags for me
while I think I'm getting points for being Dignified,
        she knows all about old men's prostates,
however good an act I put on.
        Leaving a puddle on the floor
would be a satisfying slap in her face
        for reading me like a book,
and with the long walk home ahead, a relief,
        even with wet pants leg flapping.

My lament is this,
        that any dog anytime
is free to squat
        or lift its leg to pee,

and on the street Bukowski
        or any normal freak
would simply turn to a wall and take
        a necessary leak,

which sometimes makes it seem
        that my worst mistake
was choosing
        Dignity.

You win,
        Bukowski.

AT THE LOS ANGELES COUNTY MUSEUM OF ART

(Reading, November 21, 1997)

I'm still doing it.
Not *that*, I still do that too.
I mean poetry,
I'm still at it.
After fifty years
— I can hardly believe it myself—
I'm still writing.
Still sending out my poems,
getting rejection slips—
fifty years of rejection slips,
with a few acceptances
here and there.

Why bother? Who cares?
We do.
All of us here
in this room care.
We're still doing it.

No matter what anybody says,
I'm going to go on doing it,
and as they slide my cadaver
into the furnace,
even going up in flames
I'll cry out for the world to hear,

I'M STILL DOING IT!

UNDER THE NIGHT SKY, TURNING

—adapted from "Mientras el Cielo Gire"
by Reinaldo Arenas

As long as it spins around us, this starry night,
you are my rescuer and my agony,
O magical vision,
boy in underwear, pale under the stars,
who saves me and drives me crazy
over and over again.
While this mad, brilliant night sky whirls overhead,
I've got to track every hell out there
to protect you,
while staying alive
to our every possible pleasure.
While
the great sky
wheels around us,
in you I live the truth of my poetry
and its poison dart,
the seductive thrill of danger,
the unsleeping eye and its dream—
my terror, and then the miracle.
As long as the night sky turns....
it turns for you.
You justify what I am,
with my rough trade and giddy escapes,
serious in private but publicly outrageous,
with my innocence and my guilt,
whether I choose suicide or life, whatever.
While
this night of ours
exists,
alone in the tragedy of my life,

in the total ruin of it,
I will suffer hell over you,
you, my eternal silence,
my consolation.
As long as this night exists ... ah, but does it?
Anyway,
as long
as you are
here,
you are the mirror of my time,
the forever and the moment
(O long memory and evanescence!),
my failure and the poem of it,
my enemy, my creation.
I want no other light than the light you shed,
no other ache than from your being.

O, could you really exist?

EPITAPH FOR NO GRAVE

after "Autoepitafio," by Reinaldo Arenas

Poet, whether true or phony, I can't judge,
but I was a real lunatic.
My fate was other peoples' nightmare,
and it was okay with me—I was no saint.
I believed in living on the edge or not at all.
Restless as a tomcat under the moon,
for me, ambition was meaningless,
and the routine life unbearable.
The most sordid experience I'd risk my skin for—
and risked it a thousand times,
ready to gamble everything for a beautiful boy.
But I didn't want to keep him,
just borrow him for a night
then send him home.

Jailed, treated like a leper, forced into exile,
I could still wake up grateful for another morning.
Under the worst insults humanity hurled at me,
let no one say that Arenas bowed his head.
I walked through it all, a tightrope walker
balancing in the high state of the impossible,
And when I teetered on the wire and the crowd gasped,
I fooled everybody and sailed off into the Infinite.

I don't expect a funeral, speeches, an escort of mourners.
Don't even bury me, it would drive me crazy to lie there.
Just scatter my ashes at sea
where the nervous currents will swirl them about.
But wait, I'm not through: My final wish
is for a horny youth to dive in right after me.

with thanks to Jaime Manrique

60

GLORY HOLES FOR LARRY

1927–1992

It's not only young guys dying of AIDS.
Virgil was ninety, Maurice in his eighties,
and my friend, Larry Duffy, sixty-five.

Larry's father called him "Little Wolfgang,"
he was so clever at music.
That was the trouble, he was too talented
—music, art, writing—
ever to settle down into one track
that would lead to anything.

He liked to work in factories and restaurants.
It wasn't radical politics.
He didn't have the least bit of snobbery in him.
He just preferred to spend his time with proles
and light up their lives with his chatter
than hang out in the arts scene,
where you'd think he belonged.

He was a brilliant non-stop talker.
We knew all his stories by heart—
the caption from *Life* Magazine
describing Ingrid Bergman, "fresh as a Swedish snowfall,"
and the tag lines
of his favorite *New Yorker* cartoons—
the lady at a piano concert, who says to her friend,
"He's the only one who gets the meat out of Humperdinck."
And the one during the war, where the mother
goes, oblivious, to talk to the fierce top sergeant
about her drafted son:
"His nickname's Bunny

and he responds to gentleness."
He kept doing the radio commercial,
with the folksy housewife saying,
"Have another cupcake, Mrs. Beasley. They're good!"
When he got *Sorry, Wrong Number* one Christmas,
he memorized the dialogue,
endlessly whining with Barbara Stanwyck,
"I'm a sick woman.
I need soothing, and companionship."

We both grew up in Lynbrook,
a horrible town out on Long Island,
where we were the little guys everybody beat up.
But we didn't really become friends until after the war,
when Larry was going to Juilliard on the G.I. Bill,
studying music composition, before he dropped out
into his spotty lifetime employment record.
On a new job—he could talk himself into any job—
he would charm everybody,
work like Employee of the Year
for two weeks,
and then start ignoring the alarm clock in the morning.
He also drifted in and out of several major
and several hundred minor relationships,
thousands if you count every quickie
in the Long Island Railroad johns,
where desperate commuters snatch a moment of fun
before returning to their respectable lives.

It wasn't all glory holes, though.
He lived for a long time
with a tall, handsome ex-sailor, named Bill,
stage designer at the Bucks County Playhouse.
But back in the forties and fifties,
we were all trying to go straight,
and even Larry, a man dedicated as few others
to the joys of gay sex,

got married
just long enough to have two children,
before he split.
I'm simplifying considerably,
leaving out the numerous scandals, affairs, disasters.
He finally got sensible
and settled down with another guy—
not that that straightened out the mess he was always in.

They sneaked away to Florida to escape hopeless debts,
but even there, when I'd call,
I'd hear the piano was repossessed,
or the telephone was turned off or unlisted,
or my letters would come back, "no forwarding address."
Finally, he found a steady job
in a school for the handicapped,
where the children needed him so,
that for the first time in his life
he managed to get up in the morning
for work.

Through it all, music remained his passion.
A church music director he was balling
got him to compose music for the choir,
which lasted as long as the affair did.
And during his marriage, fudging his lack of degrees,
he was taken on as music teacher at a private school,
until that blew up when the marriage did.
He used to play for me fragments
of a Menotti-like opera he was composing about his mother,
who sang arias of masochism
while she stitched blouses for her daughters.
In his last years, whenever he could
make the payments on a piano,
he perfected the sonatas of his childhood,
reeling them off like a demented Glenn Gould.

Marooned in Fort Lauderdale,
he used his left-over energies painting portraits,
crocheting enormous afghans,
and writing long illustrated letters
that we passed around.
Oddly, he never turned to drink,
but smoked like a chimney, sneered at exercise,
and lived mostly on fast food—he loved drive-ins,
though his driver's license was always being revoked
for traffic violations,
and he would get by with old out-of-state licenses.

He continued to have the morals of an alley cat,
and to the end was devoted to highway sex shops.
That was his choice, so it was inevitable
that AIDS would bring him down,
but thanks to the junk food diet
and lungs wrecked by chain smoking,
it took him mercifully fast
with the first onslaught of pneumonia.

It wasn't a wasted life.
He was the kind you go on
telling stories about
and laughing,
glad
that you were lucky enough
to know him.

AT THE GATES OF HEAVEN

Did you hear about the three nuns
who were killed
in an automobile accident?
When they appeared at the gates of heaven,
expecting to be automatically admitted,
Saint Peter said that first
they would each have to give
the correct answer to a question.
The nuns, still in shock from their accident,
looked at each other with alarm.

Nun Number One,
Saint Peter roared,
Who was the first man?

In a nervous, little voice
she answered, *Adam?*

Correct! Peter cried,
and a blast of trumpets
welcomed her into heaven.

Nun Number Two was ready to faint,
as Peter turned on her his terrible gaze,
And who was the first woman?

Eve, she answered, breathless.

Again Peter cried, *Correct!*
And the gates swung open for her, too.

By now, Nun Number Three was in a complete tizzy.
When Saint Peter asked,

And what were the first words
Eve spoke to Adam?

Nun Number Three went white as a sheet,
put her hand to her face and moaned,
Gee, that's a hard one . . .

and heavenly trumpets blared,
she sprouted wings
and in she flew.

AND GOD CREATED MICE

I was doing yoga one night
when a mouse walked across the rug calmly in front of me.
That did it. I had to act.
I baited the Have-a-Heart trap with cheese,
and caught 5 mice in 24 hours.

Once before, I had tried catching mice
with a glue trap.
When I picked up the box with the mouse inside,
its paws stuck in the glue,
it was screaming.
Such a perfect little mouse in a box,
but I had to drown it in the toilet bowl.

My brother, who loaned me the Have-a-Heart trap
understood mouse psychology.
They can't *not* go for the cheese, he said,
and once they take the bait, the trapdoors drop.
From the sound of it in the night
they are racing back and forth in the cage,
and shaking the wires with their teeth.

When I released them in the rock garden in the courtyard,
each one had its own little mouse personality
and reacted differently to being set free in the wilds.
Some scooted out of the trap,
happy to be free in the new world of outdoors.
Others were reluctant and held on,
having to be shaken from the cage.
One even stood on a rock and looked up at me.

They were all perfect little creatures
and for a moment, I considered keeping them in a big box,

and feeding them,
then said, Oh, no!
I already look crazy enough.

COUPLES SYNDROME

My mother's argument
against marrying a goy
was that sooner or later
they will call you a kike,
or a dirty Jew—
the worst thing
anyone could say.

But having lived for years with a goy
who has called me everything else,
I wonder how he could have resisted.

Like my mother, he's an Aries
and they'll say anything to win.
When my brothers infuriated her,
Ma threw whatever was in her hand,
even knives.

Loving someone doesn't mean
you don't want to kill them
by any means you can.

Collaborators

It turns into a wrangle
over every word:

I don't like anything you do
and you don't like anything I do.

꒰꒱

While I was lying awake all night
you were snoring away.

Oh yeah? Everytime I got up to pee
I heard you snoring.

꒰꒱

Stop treating me like a pet,
he complained.

That was only that day.
Sometimes he is pet
and sometimes master,

and sometimes we're two dogs
snarling at each other.

Actually, the secret of success in a relationship
is to look on your mate as a house pet—
Think of it, if they were a dog
you'd never treat them as you do.

But you're not in competition
with your dog.

꒰꒱

There was a terrible explosion
and I walked through the streets in flames,
towers leaning crazily in the sky.

War had broken out.

You were on the other side of the city
and there was no way to get over there to you
or ever find each other again.

∞

Wallace Stevens and his wife   solved their problem
            by drawing a line   through the center of the house.
    He had to stay on his side   and she on hers.

    I suspect it was her idea   and she laid down the law.

∞

Say you're one of those people
who can never get up in the morning,
even if you want to,
who just lies there in a hopeless daze,
hour after hour,

then the only solution
is to hook up with someone
who jumps out of bed every morning—
there are such people, I found one—
who makes the bed, shaves,
eats breakfast,

and whether you feel like it or not,
you'll find yourself dragging your ass out of bed,
and making him breakfast.

ॐ

Every couple has a stack of wet blankets.
Whenever one of them gets excited about something,
maybe a terrific new idea,

the rule is that the other
will grab a cold, wet blanket
and slap it over him.

ॐ

It Goes Like This

Let's do such and such!

(No answer.)

Why not?

Because.

Because why?

Because everything you think is fun,
I DON'T!

ॐ

Old couples.

The older they get
the tighter they cling,

desperate not to be
left alone.

ZLATYA'S REVENGE

adapted from the Serbian of
Vuk Stefanovic Karadzic

(NOTE: When I told a Yugoslav friend I was working on a translation of one of Vuk Karadzic's poems, he exclaimed, "Why, he's our Homer!" And indeed, Bogdan Bogdanovic called Karadzic "the great father of our nation ... who codified the Serb language in the 19th century." The following is one of the oral folk epics Karadzic recorded, which was given to me in a rough translation twenty years ago by Dr. Alexander Nejgebauer of the University of Novy Sad. I recently came across it among my papers, and in light of the outbreak of war in the Balkans after the destruction of the Yugoslav federation, the poem suddenly seemed revelatory, alarmingly so. This not-so-simple folk tale is instructive for anyone interested in the ethnic conflict. At the same time, it is modern in its irony, implicit in the "happy" ending, where the heroine, first neglected as a Moslem wife, is again put in her place on becoming a Christian, even after demonstrating that her fighting prowess is equal to any male's.)

Lady Zlatya, wife of the Aga of Udbinya,
a Moslem enclave in the Balkans,
is writing to her mother
in the distant city where she lives:

Dark was the day, mama,
you married me off
to that skunk, the Aga Hassan.
It's nine years already,
and I still don't know what a man is good for.
Everybody gets his love but me!
In summer, the Aga's off to the wars,
capturing slave girls for his pleasure.
Winters, the Aga's in the tavern with the lads,
and for all I know they get his kisses too.

Don't expect to hear from me again, mama.
Young as I am, I swear I'll hang myself
from the gatepost in the courtyard
or leap from the tower of our house
and break my miserable, still virginal neck.

Zlatya's mother reads this with alarm,
and answers at once:
I beg you, my daughter, don't,
no matter how desperate you are.
Suicide's a sin against the soul.
Just calm down and listen, darling.
Not far from where you live
is the Christian city of Seyn,
ruled by the noble Lord Ivo.
Before we married you off to the Aga,
Lord Ivo asked me and your father for your hand.
So take the advice of your mother now,
dress up fit to kill, not as a woman but as a man,
and on the Aga's prize Arabian steed,
you know the one he rides into battle on,
flee to the city of Seyn,
where the Christian Lord Ivo, I'm sure,
will be overjoyed to see you.

When Zlatya gets this letter, how she laughs
over her mother's brilliant plan.
Luckily, the Aga is not at home,
so she gets herself up exactly as the Aga does,
when he parades himself to the mosque for prayers,
in a fine green robe and trousers of cloth of gold,
and over that a radiant suit of armor
with mace and scimitar buckled at the waist.
What a magnificent sight the Lady Zlatya is
with her dark velvet brows
and nine plumes waving on the sable hat
above her flowing hair!

She stuffs a pair of goatskin saddlebags
with ducats from the Aga's treasure,
as many as they hold,
and saddles up the white Arabian horse,
the one her mother mentioned,
draping over him a golden cape,
tasseled round with gleaming coins.

As the muezzin warbles out his midnight prayer,
the Aga's Lady leaps on the lively Arab
and spurs him straight toward the mountain
that lies between Udbinya and the city of Seyn.
The clever horse is familiar with the route
since with his master, the Aga Hassan,
he often went on raids
against the Christian city.

By dawn, the Lady reaches the mountaintop,
and with the Aga's golden spyglass
looks across the valley, where distant church spires
catch the sun's first rays.
She spurs her horse down the other slope,
but just short of her goal, she's caught by nightfall,
and is forced to take lodging in a tavern
where she passes herself off as a man
and boldly quenches her thirst with wine
at a table in the public room.
The next day she arrives at Seyn
as the Christians are leaving church.

After his morning prayers, Lord Ivo of Seyn
is in the tower of his compound
already drinking with the knights of his retinue,
when the Aga's Lady on her horse
trots into the courtyard through the gates,
and there meets Ivo's mother:
Tell me, old dear, asks Zlatya,

76

after a flourish of courtesies,
have I come to Ivo's palace?
And is the master home?

Indeed, he is, answers Ivo's mother,
taking in the glittering finery of the horseman.
He's up in the tower with his knights.
But, for the love of God, young Lord, forgive me,
I can't resist asking where you come from,
and why do you ask for Ivo?

I come, replies the knight, from the Moslem zone
to visit Ivo, Lord of Seyn.
He and I are brothers under God,
but we haven't seen each other
since taking the oath of brotherhood.

The mother of Ivo picks up her skirts
and runs straight to the tower.
My son, she cries, there's a Turkish knight below
who says he's your blood brother.
I've had a long life, but never in my born days
have I seen a handsomer man.
He's dressed in such gorgeous clothes
and his Arab horse has such splendid trappings,
that the whole courtyard's sparkling with him.

Ivo barely waits to hear his mother out
before ordering his servants:
Go down and help the Turk dismount,
and ask him to come join us in the tower.

The servants rush to stable the stranger's horse,
and they lead Zlatya by her soft white hands
up to the whitewashed tower,
where she greets all the warriors in the name of God.
They greet her back with equal courtesy

and make room for her at the table,
then pour the dark red wine all round
and raise their goblets to the honored guest.

Lord Ivo of Seyn's no fool.
He knows perfectly well
this is no blood brother as he claims,
but he's as dazzled by the lovely youth
as his mother and all the others are.
After drinking until their faces are red,
Ivo addresses the mystery knight:
God be with you, stranger,
pray tell us where you're from,
and what name you're known by?

The lovely Lady answers:
I am a knight from Turkish Udbinya,
and go by the name of Osman the Albanian.
I was Ensign to that weasel, the Aga Hassan,
but I had a quarrel with him
over the dividing up of spoils.
So, as a free knight, I left the Aga,
and have come today to join you in Seyn,
for now I hate the Turkish faith
and mean to take up yours.

Ivo is thrilled and gives Zlatya a hug.
Well done, Osman the Albanian! he cries.
If this is true and you become a Christian,
you can have Angia, my sister, for your wife,
and I'll build you a whitewashed tower next to mine,
and share with you my father's lands and treasure.

Thank you, Lord Ivo, the handsome youth replies,
but I didn't come here looking for handouts.
I've got plenty of treasure of my own.
Listen, from here on in—she raises her glass—

I pledge fidelity to you, my Lord,
and vow never to deceive you.
Here, Zlatya is speaking from the heart
and doesn't consider her cross-dressing as deceit.
It's simply necessary for her purposes.
To prove her good will, the Lady asks the servants
to fetch her ducat-loaded saddlebags.
Call your treasurer, Lord Ivo, she says,
that he may put my money in your treasure room.
We'll need it for expenses,
not least, to pay for all the wine we drink.

When Ivo's treasurer has hauled away
the saddlebags of gold amid general exclamation,
Ivo embraces the Aga's Lady
and kisses her brow between her velvet eyes:
Well done, Osman the Albanian! he cries,
and lifts a glass of wine in another toast to her.

In fact, they don't stop drinking till the sabbath,
when Ivo, together with his troop of knights,
escorts Osman the Albanian to the church.
There he converts the "youth" to Christianity,
giving "him" the Christian name of Jovan
and his sister Angia's hand in marriage.
And when the dark of night descends,
to the chamber of love the bride and groom are led.
But what happens there is unexpected,
as if two devils came face to face,
recoiling one from the other.

The morning after, Ivo awakens early,
and walking around the white tower of his house,
calls up to his beloved new brother-in-law:
Yo! My Ensign Jovan,
have you risen to a peaceful morning-after?
Did my sister Angia please you?

Ensign Jovan answers:
I am fine, and feel well-satisfied,
for who could the lady fail to please?
But my Angia does seem a bit unhappy.

Hearing this, Angia's mother asks her daughter:
Tell me, little Angia,
tell your mother why you seem so sad?
Did you get a scolding from your husband, Jovan?
Or perhaps your new master doesn't please you?

Please, old mother, leave me be!
The lovely Angia stamps her foot.
Jovan doesn't mean a thing to me anymore.
He didn't caress or even scold me.
And she bursts into tears.

The old woman marches up to Ivo:
My dearest son, our Angia's in trouble!
Jovan doesn't seem to care for her.

At once, Ivo of Seyn calls in Jovan:
My sister claims you haven't touched her.
Tell me, is it true?

Master, Zlatya answers, on converting to your religion
I swore a solemn oath
not to make love
before going off to war
and proving my faith in battle.
So assign your Captain Coman to me now,
plus thirty of your trusted knights,
to help me deal with my sworn enemy,
that weasel, Hassan, the Aga of Udbinya.

Lord Ivo can hardly refuse his sister Angia's husband,
who leads her thirty warriors up the mountain,

where she dismounts and climbs a fir tree
to spy with her glass the road across the other valley.
When at last she sees her husband's familiar banner
weaving through the trees on the mountain paths,
she climbs down and announces to her band:
The Aga's coming up the mountain now
with thirty warriors from Udbinya.
Let's give them a hearty welcome.
Each of you strike at whoever's nearest him,
but don't anybody touch the Aga Hassan.
I myself want to capture that skunk alive.
I'm sure my Arab's faster than his bay.

Straight into ambush the Aga rides,
and thirty Christian muskets fire,
killing half his escort right away.
At once, the Christians draw their sharpened steel
and cut off all the enemies' heads.
Only the Aga manages to escape,
pursued by his Lady on the Arab horse.
Down the mountainside she chases hard,
till she catches up with him in a cul-de-sac
and wallops him with her mace,
a blow that knocks him from his saddle.
Leaping on top of the stunned and fallen Aga,
she ties his hands, jumps on his bay,
and leading her own horse by the bridle,
parades the Aga on foot before her back to camp.

With a cry of victory,
she shows the Aga to her comrades,
and awards his horse as prize to Captain Coman.
Then, they all set out again for Seyn,
sending an emissary ahead to announce the news:
O Lord Ivo, the rider says,
your Ensign Jovan has done the job
and is bringing the Aga back alive,

with the heads of thirty enemy knights.
He begs you to grant him one request.
But what that is
he wants to ask of you himself.

When the convoy enters the city gates,
the Lord of Seyn calls out, Well done, Jovan!
You have proved yourself a mighty hero!
Now tell me, what do you want?

Thank you, Master, replies the Lady,
on her knees before him.
Take all the booty as my gift to you,
but I beg you—
and here she rose to her feet with flashing eyes—
give me that weasel, the Aga Hassan,
and a sturdy rope to hang him with!

Ivo is dazed by the fiery beauty of the youth
and grants the favor with a nod.
Away the Lady leads the Aga Hassan,
and when they reach the riverbank, she speaks:
Listen to me, Hassan,
do you realize who's about to hang you?
I may be the man they call the Ensign Jovan,
but I am also Zlatya, your wife. Remember?
Nine years have passed, my husband,
since you bought me from my parents
and you did not kiss me once in all that time.

So she hangs the Aga with the rope,
and returning at once to Ivo, Lord of Seyn, confesses:
O my master, I never was Osman the Albanian,
but the Lady of the fallen Aga Hassan,
and I've come to you to be your wife.

Ivo is overjoyed,

and leads the lovely Lady to the whitewashed church,
but just in case she thought
she'd go on drinking in the tower with his men
matching their tales of valour with her own,
he has her christened again,
this time with the name of Modest Rose,
after which he marries her, and with the Aga's ducats
orders a fabulous wedding feast
to which he invites all his gentlemen.

CANNIBAL BEACH

I heard that the wide beach of my childhood
has been almost washed away, even the wild dunes
of nearby cannibal beach,
famous for gay hanky panky in the reeds,
and waterfront drag shows fathers took their children to
"if they promised to be good"—
an arena of sex and fun,
battered by years of storms
and even the unnoticeable wear and tear
of wavelets we once frisked bare-ass in,
watching for the police.

We were always watching for the police,
and you never could be sure when you reached for a prick
that he wasn't a dick and handcuffs
wouldn't be snapped on you.
It used to cost a couple of hundred
for the lawyer to pay off the judge.

When I discovered cannibal beach,
I'd ride my bicycle the ten miles from home—
"what I did for love," as the song goes.
There, in early summer, needle-beaked birds
would swoop, whistling, to drive me away
from their chicks, invisible in the sand.

Behind the dunes I came upon
the beer-bellied Irishman of my dreams,
clutching his fat prick in the bullrushes.
He put my bike in the trunk of his car, parked
where half the cars had sunk carelessly up to the axle
while their owners wandered through the reeds,
and drove me home to his house in Queens,

where holy pictures on the walls
and a wedding photo of stiff parents
watched us from the dresser,
as they would for many a year,
mess up their chenille bedspread.

TO MY COUNTRY

after Ra'hel

I've never praised you in my poems,
and what I have written
will bring you little glory.
But frankly, those who wave the flag
are scary.

And what is to praise?
Here, in your most anarchic of cities,
a stony landscape where it's just possible
for my kind to survive,
I have planted myself like a tree,
whose branches are filled with the cries
of suffocating birds.

But if I don't sing your praises,
you obviously don't need me either,
and I admit my gifts are modest.
Still, the lucky ones you reward
seem even less gifted
though good at playing the literary/
political game.
You prefer them boring,
and tame.

You don't take any more notice of me
than you do of the poor
collapsed on the sidewalks.
Poetry is not supposed to mention them,
or the leaders who live in luxury
and blame the poor for being poor.

Poetry, your literary critics agree,
is supposed to be about language.

So I'm out of luck—
my poems are about people.
For me, the whole purpose of poetry these days
is to point out the stoniness of your soul,
especially since you
sing your own praises plenty.

Still, indifferent to me as you are,
here is my life offering, my poetry,
that in another country, another time,
would probably get me thrown into jail,
so I have to thank you, after all,
for neglect, for obscurity.

THE SPIRIT OF '76

"Time rushes like a madman forward ..."
—*John Berryman*

The first twenty-four years of this century
      were not mine,
and though at my age it's foolhardy

to assume survival even until tomorrow,
      by the year two thousand
I'll be an ancient, or a ghost, of seventy-six.

So I'll risk a millennial goodbye in advance
      to the century I was born in, an alien,
and lived through, a klutz.

The Depression made me, the saddest little Jewboy,
      then the War and the Holocaust.
I really want to leave him behind and exit laughing.

Goodbye, then, to my youth, and worse, my hair.
      Nice cock though, and still trim from yoga.
Anybody want a clean old man?

Forget it,
      who could have predicted AIDS....
Goodbye, with regret, to dirty stuff.

My parents have faded away at last.
      I survived you two sickos, just,
but it's a relief to say thanks, and goodbye.

And to the Cold War, McCarthy, and HUAC,
      which burned out our brains,
good riddance and feh!

It's the only explanation for the country
        falling for cadavers like Reagan
and Bush...Feh! Feh! The stink hangs on.

Trying to take in the stink of
        the collapse of the Soviet Union,
I wave goodbye with an ache

to all my crazy ideals and illusions,
        more fascinated than terrified
as the predicted monsters rise out of the wreckage.

I wish the worst would wait till I'm gone,
        but if even the IMF is getting nervous
it's all-passengers-to-lifeboat-stations.

It's bye-bye time already
        as friends die off from age and AIDS,
so if I'm not ready now to let it go I'll never be.

Goodbye, then, to all my years on earth, mostly wasted
        except for sexy moments in the dark,
cooking for you, sweetheart,

and especially poetry, fantasy weapon
        for non-fighters, losers, and sissies.
I'll settle for it and Spanish brandy

to face the new century, which, like programming a VCR,
        no seventy-six year old twentieth century man
can be expected to understand a thing about,

and when anything I have to say, like
        "Did I ever tell you about the time in the War...?,"
will produce a yawn.

A MAN AND HIS PENIS

*"The only happy man is he who is at one
with his cock."*
                              —*Socrates*

1

Someone said
he had a lover's quarrel
with the world.

They can say about me,
that all my life
I've had a lover's quarrel
with my prick.

2

When I was young I suffered from fear
of The Terrible Shrinking Disease,
afflicting half of Asia.

But what I dreaded never happened.
It got bigger, it got smaller,
leading to my mature acceptance of the fact
that it has a mind of its own.

But I still can't help feeling
that someday we could get together.

Like the pessimist-optimist controversy,
some days I look on the positive side
and am contented,

on others I curse my fate,
and especially the circumciser
who deprived me of the vital centimeters.

I would have loved my foreskin,
and feel that this particular sacrifice
was more than God
should ask a man for.
But whoever said being a Jew was easy?
So perhaps it was necessary
to establish that right off.

You schmuck, God roars,
what are you complaining about?
I gave you a nice handful, didn't I?

Anyway, I suspect that a real man
thinks his prick
the perfect size.

3

PARADOX

The sleeping man
is the man
with the hard-on,
the dreamer is the man
with a hard-on
all night.

His whole life
was a struggle
not to have
a hard-on,
a struggle

to get out of
bed.

But the man
who is dreaming
is the man
with the hard-on

not the waking man
who has struggled
for years
to get out of bed.

4

ADDICT

as
some people
confess
to being
two martinis
short
of
normal

I'm
two puffs
on a joint
away
from being
a man with
a
terrific
cock

5

SURVEY

Do you have a big one?
No, but it's a horny little bastard.

Sir, do you have a big one?
Search me, it's got a life of its own.

And you, sturdy lad, do you have a big one?
When it gets up to its dirty tricks,
nobody complains.

And how about you, young man?
Hard as a rock, you'd love it.

You up there on the scaffolding,
would you say you have a big one?
Yeh, go down on it, motherfucker.

Forgive me for interrupting, gentlemen,
but do you have a big one?
It's perfect.
And you sir?
I don't know, but I'm very attached to it.

Hi, fella, got a big one?
Yes, and it's hungry
for your asshole, baby.

6

HIS FINEST HOUR

It's bigger than he is, I heard,
as I woke up in the barracks,
one hot Sunday morning

in Texas.

A group of soldiers
were standing around my bunk
where I was lying
naked on my back,
on the verge
of a wet dream,
cock rock hard
and pulsing,
ready to shoot.

Hey! I yelled,
and pulled the sheet up just in time,
as the guys walked away,
grinning.

7

OLD ACQUAINTANCE

> *"Deirdre! Come out!*
> *Come out from behind that screen.*
> *I've been hiding behind screens*
> *since before you were born."*
> *—Bette Davis, in "Old*
> *Acquaintance"*

Old friend, we've come through
in pretty good shape, so far,
better, in fact,
than during those angst-filled years
when you wrecked my life
and I wrecked yours. Remember?
But, back then, we didn't appreciate each other,
did we—like an ill-matched couple,

a bad job by an incompetent marriage broker,
or who just got married out of general horniness
rather than any real compatibility.

I never liked your looks or size
and you had ideas of your own
I couldn't figure out,
though I responded to your goading
and roamed the nights away.
My God, what you led me into,
and I got you into some pretty tight fixes myself.

Life is less strenuous now.
In our golden years, you make few demands.
We've both come to like a bit of a wank,
with none of the old recriminations after.
And I've even learned to admire,
as I pose in the mirror,
your silky length,
respect your sulky independence.
I wonder that I ever thought you
insufficient, myself under-endowed—
or else you've grown.

Best of all, I'm impressed
by how good we look together—
the proportions seem just right.
So, Good Cock,
dick, prick, dong,
lul, bitte, schwantz,
wang, willie, weenie,
and all your other names,
if you've a mind to, now,
and I'd say you've earned it,
stand up, old friend, with me
and take a bow.

GETTING TO KNOW YOU

Like the hard-on,
the asshole is another level of being.
It's me, but a me
even I must negotiate with,
especially when washing after shitting,
as civilized life demands.
For it does not allow the soapy finger in,
presenting an impenetrable surface.

Do not be misled.
It is offering the coy resistance
it would to a lover. Therefore,
with a lover's singlemindedness,
remain stalwart in seeking entrance,
probe for a crevice
until the fingertip,
with a delicate wiggle,
pries open the curl of muscle
and slips in,

and miraculously, you will find
that the whole organ relents,
goes soft for the soaping,
with a sappy grin.

WHEN I WAS A DOG

1

"No dog ever invited another dog
to share its lunch."
— *Baghwan*

Ah, if only young men
were like dogs
that bound over,
wagging their tails.

Their wet tongues
licking you,
they'd only want love,

not the kind with wary eyes
that snarl
if you reach out
to stroke them.

2

"Mens got dawg in 'em."
— *Ntozake Shange*

Their devotion to us
is a mystery.
Are they studying up on us?

People obsessed with animals—
cat people, dog lovers—

could have been assigned the role
of protecting them
to prepare them
for future lives as humans.

When I massage my scalp
I seem to remember
when I was a dog,

or the head remembers being a dog's,
and how delicious it was
to be patted and stroked,
and how I still need it desperately.

3

Power Source

Like harnessing
the tides
or the wind,
how about attaching
dogs' tails
to power generators?

I want the job
of patting the dog
to keep its tail
wagging!

We'll illuminate
whole cities,
countries—
together, we'll
light up the world!

DECRYPTING THE MESSAGE

It came to me in the bathroom
while looking at myself in the mirror.
The message just shot into my mind:
RECLAIM THE TOP.

I first assumed it referred to my baldness,
that the trick of growing hair again,
of interest to every man,
was to reclaim a distant,
a neglected, part of me—
the top of my head.

But I'm not at all sure,
because now comes another message—
this time to reclaim the bottom
as well as the top.
The latest instructions seem to mean,
once you have the bottom,
you can get back the top.
And the top, as Cole Porter says,
is defined by the bottom, as in,
"Darling, if I'm the bottom, you're the top."
Though there I'm sure that Cole's
referring to sexual roles.
Amazing that we once thought
popular songs were about
something fuzzy called "romance."

Only in a limited sense, then,
do the messages mean
to take back
my hair above,
and my cock below,

both half-relinquished
in life's struggle,
as I've withdrawn over the years
from both top and bottom
and clenched myself, fist-like,
in the center.

But the top referred to
may, in fact, be somewhere
"out there" beyond me—
it shifts around all the time.
A solid bottom seems basic, though,
and reclaiming it possible,
like learning to stand on the whole
bottom of your feet.

Amazing how "they" keep giving me
more work to do,
keep setting me
all these instructions to ponder.
Especially since I don't actually know
what any of this means,
or who "they" are.
But they certainly like the bathroom mirror
to tune in on me.

And it's not necessary
to know what it means.
The beautiful message remains,
RECLAIM THE TOP
and stand tall.

DEATH MASK

"Old age is the most unexpected
of all the things that happen to a man."
— *Leon Trotsky.*

"Do not let me hear
Of the wisdom of old men, but rather of their
 folly,
Their fear...."
— *"East Coker," by T. S. Eliot*

1

In the mirror now,
        what I see
reminds me
        I won't be here forever.

I don't feel like
        that face at all.
Inside it, I protest,
        I'm quite different.

It's somebody's grandfather,
        not me.

Whose grandfather is that?
        I don't want him.

2

Ah, memory, memory....

terrible,

to be losing

the words.

3

How do you get from here to there—
I mean, from where I am
to the nursing home?
In a snap of the fingers,
the blink of an eye.

Like my mother said,
as she was being loaded
into the ambulance,
It went so fast.

4

Life
      a lazy buzz,
then
      the quick sting.

A long inward breath,
      then
the sudden
      exhaling.

LIVING WILL

For Diane Derrick

All is ready for the final event:
The will is in the top left drawer of the chest
along with instructions about cremation.
It's quite relaxing, really,
to have one's affairs in order,
except for last minute things.

I am as prepared as I can get, I think,
except for the inevitable final panic
before the breathing stops—
that must be a terrifying moment.
But what bliss,
as life fades away,
to let it all go.

Please follow my instructions
not to resuscitate,
or keep me alive as a medical case.
It's not acceptable to me
and would be an unnecessary burden on you.

Much will be left in your hands.
Forgive me, but it is unavoidable,
the mess.
I leave all the money to you,
a small consolation,
but please send my oriental carpets to my sister
who was always my co-conspirator in the family.

My chief qualm is that I am leaving you
my literary works to deal with.

I'm used to the literary world
after fifty years of it—
submissions,
the long waits for editorial decision,
the rejections, or publication
in an obscure journal several years later.
It's hardly worth it
unless it's your own career you are building.

But promoting a dead poet
can be an amusing hobby.
Poetry is a posterity sweepstakes
and who knows which horse will come in.
I suspect I'll be hard to overlook
in a field of forgettables.
Even the big boys: Nobody
will want to read them after they're gone,
except scholars.

Here I am, facing oblivion,
but still obsessed with my career,
a foolishness I've never grown out of.
It's an obsession, poetry
and the world of poetry
the hornets' nest or bees in a bonnet,
that nobody else gives a damn about.

That's what so attractive about it.

I could never have done
anything else with my life.
And along with it, devotion
to a friend who needed me.
Hopefully, he has died before me
so I need not regret abandoning him
to the difficulties of a single life.

But should he survive me,
I know that you, his dear sister,
his closest other,
will look after him.
He is my main reason for grief
at leaving the world.

But I can't say my farewells just yet,
my memoirs still need a lot of work,
and I've got to finish
my new manuscript of poetry.
May death take me
only as I put down
the last word.

EPITAPH

Jerk, loser, fuck up,
    schlemiel, sad sack, twit,
I stumbled over my shadow
    and fell in a lake of shit.

THE AGE OF AIDS

Our postman Jim was always after me
to sleep with him
when I came down for the mail.

He'd lower his voice thrillingly
and say, Wanna do it?

Uh-huh, I'd say, unable to turn him down.
He was big
and handsome as a bronze god.

I liked to practice my Dutch on him.
He was from Aruba which belongs to Holland,
and called Dutch the mother tongue.
But he also spoke German
from when he was stationed in Germany,
and all the Caribbean languages as well.

You have to be overqualified
to deal with a large complex like my building,
full of struggling artists of one kind or another,
all ready to blame the mailman.
But Jim ran our mailroom like a corporate executive,
and I always told him he could do anything.
In fact, he worked part-time in a law office
where his boss wanted to send him to study law,
but he had his own ideas.
He was always going down to Brazil,
and planned to retire there
when he got his pension from the post office.
He had it all worked out—
he'd already bought land.

When? he would whisper, looking at me intently,
Come on, tell me, when?
and I'd stammer an excuse and stagger away,
breathing hard.

I could hardly mind
that he went for an old guy like I am.
It's not often anymore
that someone comes on to me,
though a man did at a party recently.
We were at the eats table
and he kept squeezing his crotch
and talking dirty,
his eyes taking a bead on me like Jim's
that made my body start vibrating.
But when he went to get another drink,
I slipped out.

Jim said he preferred Brazil
where people just went ahead and did it,
not think so much about it, like Americans.
But I was too scared and kept putting him off,
until he got really mad
and stopped talking to me.

After that, I started seeing him
waiting after work
for the head of security in our building,
a smooth, brownskinned man named Ron,
who presided over the lobby
with the kind of style that if he were white
would have gotten him a lot further
than the reception desk.
But at least he had a grown daughter
who was going to college.

My friend Tobias was always asking Ron

if he was gay,
and Ron would just laugh.
We knew, though,
and saw him leaving
with the big, handsome postman after work.
I was relieved
that Jim wasn't after me anymore.

I had been corresponding for a long time
with a composer in California named Charlie Buel,
who was setting some of my poems
to music.
Charlie would write me long letters
going into the technicalities,
as if I understood music theory like he did,
but more interesting, giving the details of his sex life,
which, considering that he had AIDS by then,
was extensive—it didn't slow him down at all.
In the sex clubs and pay parties Charlie went to
he said it was assumed everyone was positive.
But it sounded to me like they let you know
after sex, not before.
My friend Reinhard in Berlin got AIDS
from his boyfriend, Stanley, who never told him
until Reinhard came down with it himself,
and now Reinhard is also dying.

As an old man, I had to admire
Charlie's careless spirit of living
when you have accepted inevitable Death,
when you have no choice.
Old age is pretty much the same,
with the end in sight.
I asked him to compose music for a piece I wrote
inspired by his letters—a stomp
for a male group with KS lesions,
led by an old man like me

who learns from the young guys of the chorus
how to live to the end,
maybe not to go ahead and just do it,
like Jim and like Charlie,
but with spirit.

2❧

Suddenly, Jim went on sick leave,
and we learned he had AIDS too—
from all those trips to Brazil, we figured.
Capable to the end, he killed himself.
He'd been the perfect,
the unforgettable, postman,
inhabiting his steamy mailroom
like a Nubian wrestler.
An executive-type Nubian/Aruban.

Then Ron wasn't at the reception desk anymore.
He was sick, they said, over his crackhead brother.
He'd told me that someone had called him on the phone
and said that his brother was dead,
and Ron gave a great wail, and collapsed.
Later, he learned it was only someone playing a dirty trick,
but Ron seemed to shrink down after that,
and when he didn't come in anymore,
we started putting it all together
with his going home after work
with the irresistible postman.

There are new people at the front desk now,
and someone else in the mailroom
who can cope pretty well
with the difficult artists in the building.
My friend Charlie has also died,
his frantic pursuit of love over.
He lived his life to the end,

and I could never have told him not to.
But, I wonder, how do young people manage nowadays?

Charlie never lived to compose my stomp
that I meant for us all,
the cautious old and the gonad-driven young:

For Jim and Charlie, dead,
for Ron in St. Vincent's,
and for Reinhard, dying in Berlin,

A STOMP

(For an old man, and a backup group of young
men with KS lesions on their faces)

OLD MAN
It's all up with me, boys,

(The young group circles him, rhythmically stamping and clapping,
with cries of Hey, hey! Who cares? Quit whining! Let's hear it! Loud
and clear!, etc.)

OLD MAN
and nothing I can do about it,
nothing I can do about it.

GROUP
Hey, hey!
There's nothing to be done about it,
nothing to be done about it.

(More rhythmic stamping and clapping, with cries of What a relief!
Let's hear it again, etc.)

GROUP

It's all up with us, boys,
and nothing to be done about it,
nothing to be done about it.

OLD MAN

Hey, hey!
(*He dances around the group, clapping*)
And nothing I can do about it,
nothing I can do about it.

GROUP

It's all up with us, my boys,
and nothing we can do about it,
and nothing we can do about it.

(*All, including the old man, stamp and clap in rhythm, with cries of,
No time for tragedy, Live till you die, etc.*)

ALL

(*After final vigorous stomping, shout together*)
HEY, HEY!

SILVER WINGS

Notes for a Screenplay

with thanks to Neil Derrick

SILVER WINGS
Notes for a Screenplay

1995,
and Jeff, an American, is in London
for the fiftieth anniversary of V-E Day.
During World War II
he was stationed on an airfield in England,
but the day the war ended,
none of the military personnel were allowed off base,
so at last he can join in the celebrations—
in Hyde Park a pavilion has been erected
for a mammoth show.

Back in 1945,
Jeff, twenty years old and a 2nd Lieutenant,
was flying as navigator in one of the Flying Fortresses
that day after day in their thousands
took off from English air bases
to carpet-bomb the cities of Germany.
Jeff believed in what he was doing,
though the goal of the bombing was somewhat ambiguous—
it wasn't just hitting factories and rail yards and troop trains,
but was meant to demoralize the population
and shorten the war.
And why not punish ordinary Germans, he thought,
for their robot-like devotion
to that madman Hitler,
who was out to conquer the world
and set up the Germans as the master race,
with slave labor battalions and death camps
for everyone else?

Before leaving for London and the V-E anniversary
Jeff wrote to the old address in Oklahoma
of his former airplane mechanic, Moose,
whom he hadn't seen since the end of the war,
fifty years before,
to ask if the sergeant still had any snapshots of his crew.
But a letter came back from his wife
informing him that Moose was dead
and enclosed the only photo she could find,
one of Lieutenant Jeff and her sergeant husband together,
that she said her husband always carried in his wallet.

It was a snapshot of Moose,
a young, open-faced GI with sergeant's chevrons
on the sleeves of his mechanic's coveralls,
and 20-year-old Jeff, slender and too young-looking
for the gold lieutenant's bars on his shoulders
and the silver wings on his chest.
Posed in front of a B-17
both men smiled at the camera,
an arm across each other's shoulders.

Jeff remembered it was taken just after VE-Day
before he was sent back to the States
and brought back vividly
his months on the airfield in the English Midlands,
the missions over Germany he flew,
passes to shabby, wartime London,
and the lifelong ache he's carried around
for the lanky aircraft mechanic from Oklahoma.

❧

A bombing run over Munich.
In the nose of a B-17,
cradled in the roar of four engines,
Jeff is huddled over his desk

116

with his navigation instruments around him,
trying to write legibly in his log,
as explosions of anti-aircraft shells bounce the plane around
and jiggle his pen over the page,
while jagged fragments of flak
rip through the aluminum fuselage,
ricocheting around him in the nose compartment.

Jeff is bulky in his flying clothes—
an electric suit against the cold of 33,000 feet,
coveralls, flak jacket, and parachute harness.
Under his fur helmet with earphones,
his nose and mouth are covered with an oxygen mask,
and to keep in touch with the crew,
a built-in microphone
that Jeff wraps in a condom before take off
to keep it from icing up with his breath.

When he was an enlisted man,
Jeff had applied for aviation cadet training
to escape from the boredom of a clerical job
in a vast Air Force headquarters in the mid-west.
He saw himself as a fighter pilot,
so it was an irony
that he ended up at a desk in the sky.
By the military logic
that assigns cooks to building bridges
and engineers to the mess hall kitchen,
his math scores were high,
and that week the Air Force were short on navigators.

From 33,000 feet,
unreal is the vast, clear Bavarian landscape
with the snow-covered Alpine ranges to the south,
and far below, the miniature city of Munich,
pocked with columns of smoke,
as the file of American bombers

wheels around the city in a wide arc,
waiting their turn over the bombing run
to drop their explosives.
Whatever tragedies were happening down on street level
where people lived their lives, cowering in shelters,
they were far away from Jeff, five miles up,
and unrelated to the pulling
of the bombs-away switches in the American planes.

Besides navigation and record keeping,
Jeff has two machine guns,
one on either side of the "cheeks" of the plane,
in case enemy fighters attack,
but the German Luftwaffe
has been mostly destroyed by then
or grounded by lack of fuel,
and out the windows around him
he only sees the other planes of his squadron
flying wing tip to wing tip in tight formation,
with dark puffs of antiaircraft shells
exploding under them, causing the plane
to buck like a horse.

On the short bombing run over the heart of Munich—
Jeff notes the time in his log—
with Chuck the pilot holding the plane as steady as he can
through the turbulence in the air,
the bombardier in the plastic nose cone of the plane
within arm's reach of Jeff
is hunched over the bombsight with its cross-hairs,
waiting for the signal from the lead plane in the squadron
to drop another load of bombs on the target—
no pinpoint bombing
but calculated to obliterate
a square mile of the city below.

When the bomb bay doors open

is the tensest moment of all,
with the anti-aircraft fire at its heaviest.
Fear is indistinguishable from excitement,
and Jeff's hand, writing in his log,
is almost out of control.

The instant their bombardier sees the bombs fall
from the lead plane ahead of them,
he pulls his switch,
and Jeff checks his chronometer for the time.
He also notes in his log with shaking fingers
that one of their planes has been hit
and is dropping out of formation,
and more sickeningly,
that another spirals down with a trail of smoke,
and no parachutes floating free.
"Navigator to pilot," he says over the intercom,
and gives the heading home,
signing off with "Over and out."

~

Arriving back at the air base in the Midlands,
the bomber crew jumped out of the plane,
joshing each other in relief.
After eight hours in the air,
Jeff walked off wobbly onto solid ground,
as aircraft mechanic Moose, in greasy coveralls by the hangar,
whistled at the plane full of holes.
"Another one for the junkyard, lieutenant?" he called.
"Did you navigate it right into the flak?"
Jeff grinned at him, instantly refreshed.
"That's what they teach you at navigation school," he said.

He particularly liked Moose's
long, homely face with its big jaw,
and his straight, light-brown hair that blew

over his forehead.
His eyes squinted into the light
with something Scandinavian, or Indian, in them.
Moose had big, square hands,
and even in the greasy coveralls
he was a loose-jointed, wholesome animal.

After turning in his guns to Ordnance,
Jeff followed the crew into a Nissen hut
for interrogation about the mission.
When his turn came, the intelligence officers
pushed a tray of shot glasses
and a bottle of scotch across the table,
as Jeff deciphered his log for them
with its almost unreadable writing,
the seismograph of a neurological catastrophe.
Afterwards, he carried two shots of scotch outside
to drink with Moose.
It had become a ritual of theirs
that Jeff looked forward to.
On his last furlough before shipping overseas,
Moose had gotten married to his sweetheart in Oklahoma.
He would always tell Jeff if he got a letter,
and show him pictures of Cherry and the baby.
He'd kiss them both,
and swing himself on the wing of the plane
with a rebel war whoop.

After every three missions or so, Jeff got a pass,
and this time he was going to London.
The old-style second-class railroad cars
had compartments, each with its own door to the platform,
and he found one with a free place on one of the plush seats,
where he fitted himself in, elbow to elbow,
his knees nearly touching the person opposite
who held up a large newspaper before him,
murmuring "Sorry" to his neighbors as he turned the pages—

120

otherwise no one in the compartment said a word.
Two hours later Jeff was checking into a room
at the American Officers Club near Piccadilly Circus,
where in the early darkness, darker for the blackout,
whores were patrolling the grimy building arcades.

That evening, having a beer in a crowded pub,
Jeff was exchanging looks
with a tall Canadian soldier in beret and combat boots,
when he was hailed by some fellow officers from the base,
inviting him to go to a party,
but Jeff made out that he had a date already.
In a sense, he had....
With a last significant look at the Canadian
Jeff, his knees trembling, finished his beer
and stepped into the blacked-out street.
Suddenly the Canadian was beside him at the curb
where they engaged in the usual hearty ritual
about being stood up by their dates, and were they hot.
Jeff pretended not to have a place for the night,
and went with the Canadian soldier
to his hotel room.
But even after they were in bed together,
Jeff kept up the pretense
of being just a normally horny guy
and even after they started fooling around
still wouldn't let the Canadian kiss him.
But then the sex got serious
and neither of them bothered
putting on an act anymore.

Afterward, when the Canadian snuggled up
with his arms around him and started to go to sleep,
Jeff pulled away and got dressed, stammering
that he had to get back to the base.
Ignoring the soldier's disappointment,
he returned to his room at the Officers' Club,

121

relieved to be alone.
He never felt quite clean after something like that,
and spent a long time in the showers.

At the air base the next weekend,
an officers' dance was held in the mess hall
with English girls bussed in from town.
They exclaimed in wonder
over the spread laid on for them,
food they hadn't seen for years.
Jeff danced most of the evening
with a pale, pretty girl named Pauline,
and made a half-hearted attempt to get her to fuck with him,
but was relieved when she wouldn't,
because, she said, she wasn't that kind of girl.
Pauline's friend Rita was.
She danced only with Chuck, the pilot of Jeff's crew,
and slipped out with him to the officers' barracks
along with a lot of couples.

Pauline was upset about her friend,
and Jeff kept Pauline company in the mess hall,
while she waited for Rita to return.
When the military bus was announced
that would take the women back to town
and Rita hadn't returned yet,
Pauline begged Jeff to go look for her.

Inside Jeff's barracks, the lights were off
and couples were making love on the bunks.
Chuck had the bunk next to his
and Jeff could see just enough to spot
Rita and him still going at it.
He hated to interfere,
but he called out from the doorway
that the bus was leaving
and a moment later, Rita went racing by him,

buttoning her blouse and smoothing her tangled hair,
not bothering about her stockings hanging down.

୨ꝺ

At the PX, Jeff was in line
for his weekly candy and cigarette rations.
Ahead of him, Moose was putting on
a queer act for some buddies,
mincing with limp wrist to general laughter.
The soldier in the line behind Jeff
called out, "Get her, Mary!"
and winked at Jeff.
But Jeff looked vague, uncomfortable
with the guy's assumption,
and pretended not to know what he meant.
What he did with guys sometimes
was just fooling around,
like the kids he'd jacked off with in school.
When the psychiatrist in the Army Induction Center
had asked him if he liked girls,
he knew enough to answer, "Yes."
It was no lie, he liked girls,
he really did.

After Jeff got his rations at the counter,
a carton of cigarettes and a box of candy bars,
the soldier from the line caught up
and introduced himself as Ralph.
He worked in Special Services, he said,
arranging base activities.
A corporal named Tony joined them
and Ralph introduced him as the Chaplain's assistant,
rolling his eyes meaningfully.
Jeff got the message
that the Chaplain's office and Special Services
were posts for people "like that."

On signal, Ralph and Tony, like a comedy team,
took powder puffs from their shirt pockets
and powdered their noses in unison,
which Jeff found hilarious,
but tried to suppress his giggles
and studied the sawdust on the floor.
The openness of their act in the PX alarmed him
and, hoping that Moose or the other guys hadn't noticed,
he escaped to the Officers' Club.

Pauline, the English girl from the dance,
invited Jeff to her family home for dinner.
He brought cans of luncheon meat and butter,
impressing her parents.
They kept apologizing for the meager roast,
and piled most of it on his plate—
it must have been their whole meat ration for the week.
It was obvious to Jeff
that the family saw him as their daughter's boyfriend,
and he was flattered, but a little uncomfortable—
he thought he was just making friends
with a British family,
something like the pen pal
he had once corresponded with in Denmark.
But he really liked Pauline
and wanted to see her again.

In the morning, another mission,
starting with a briefing of the crews.
Moose, on the wing gassing up the plane,
asked him if he'd bring him
a piece of flak as a souvenir for his wife.
It was a daylong mission to Berlin, always a rough ride,
and on his return Jeff picked up
some jagged fragments of steel
from the floor of the cabin.
But Moose was off duty,

and he went over to Moose's barracks
to give him the flak.
There was nobody around
so he poked his head into the latrine
where several soldiers were showering in the steamy room.
Unselfconsciously soaping their naked bodies before him,
they told him that Moose was at the dance.

The enlisted men were having their turn with the local girls,
and in the cleared mess hall,
Moose was in the center of a circle,
jitterbugging with an English girl.
But as an officer Jeff was out of place,
and after the twelve-hour haul to Berlin he was dropping,
so with the help of a couple of drinks at the officer's club,
he hit the sack and passed out.

At the next officers' dance,
Pauline hinted to Jeff that she was ready
to go with him to his barracks,
but he didn't pick up on her signals.
He'd never done it with a woman,
only necked with girls in school,
and he was afraid to try—and fail.
She was obviously disappointed
when he said he had to get some sleep
if he was going to fly in the morning.
In the dark barracks, he lay alone on his bunk
and listened to the couples making out.
Across from him, Captain Chuck was with Rita,
and after he took her to the bus,
he came back and sat on the edge of Jeff's bunk
and told him how crazy he was about her.

Jeff decided that on his next pass to London,
he would pick up a whore
and see if he could fuck a woman.

Under the darkened arcades in Piccadilly Circus
everything was on offer,
though it was hard to see what you were getting.
Jeff shook off several over-painted whores with high
        pompadours,
but finally got up his nerve and responded to a woman
who seemed pleasant and motherly, rather than gaudy.
"A pound for a quickie, luv,"
she said in a cockney accent.

He went to her shabby room nearby
where she started pulling off her dress and girdle,
leaving on her stockings and garter belt.
"For an extra quid
you can stay all night," she said, lying back,
inviting him with a smile showing crooked teeth.
But her flabby body repelled him,
and on the sagging bed it was a disaster.
She diddled him a bit, his dick shrinking away,
then, obviously weary, she gave up.
"Next time, luv, don't have so much to drink,"
she said with a yawn,
and turned over and went to sleep.
On the way down the stairs, another whore
was coming up, laughing with a GI,
whose hard on was visible in his pants,
making Jeff feel more of a failure.
Back in his spartan room at the officers' hostel,
he punched the pillow in self-disgust.

He returned to the air base the next day
to find it in pandemonium.
That morning, German fighters
had flown over at treetop level
to avoid the radar,
and shot up the squadron that was just taking off
on the day's mission.

They had knocked out half a dozen American aircraft,
some already in the air and some still on the ground.
A lot of men were killed and wounded,
and with several crews out of commission
Jeff had to work a double set,
missions to Essen and Duisberg in the industrial Ruhr,
where the Germans threw up their heaviest flak,
twice to Hamburg, and twice more to Berlin,
getting back to the base in planes
that were so shot up
they were only good for scrap.
He was so tired,
he didn't linger to see if Moose was around,
and after a few whisky sours at the officers' club
tumbled into bed, only to get up
for the next morning's briefing.

But on his next pass to London, Jeff found himself
in the same train compartment
as Moose and a couple of his GI buddies.
Jeff couldn't move over next to Moose—
it would have looked funny to be too friendly
with an enlisted man,
though Moose called "Hey, Lieutenant,"
a couple of times, and when they all separated in Kings Cross
        station,
said, "See you at the Water Rat."
Jeff knew the bar off Picadilly Circus,
full of Allied servicemen.

Instead of going to the Officers' Club,
Jeff checked into the Canadian soldier's hotel,
hoping he wouldn't run into him.
That night, in the crowded Water Rat pub,
Jeff saw Moose drinking with his buddies across the bar.
He had given up hope of getting together with Moose
and was about to move on to another pub,

when a doodle bug hit nearby.
The pub shook with the explosion, and the lights went out.
Chaos.
Sirens.
Confusion in the darkness.
Outside, in the crowd escaping from the pub
Jeff and Moose stood near each other, shaken up,
watching the fire wardens' hoses
play on a burning building down the street.
The shock of the near miss
had given Moose a ravenous appetite
and he and Jeff went to eat at the Lyons Corner House nearby,
where, over rarebits, beans, and tea,
Moose dug out the latest pictures of his wife and baby,
with his usual little rebel yell of appreciation
as he studied each one.
Then Jeff handed him the flak fragment across the table.
"Oh, I forgot all about it," Moose said,
examining the sharp, jagged pieces of steel
from the exploding anti-aircraft shells over Essen.
"Deadly little buggers.
Gotta watch out for those, Lieutenant,"
he said with his irresistible grin,
his lank hair that had grown out of its regulation cut
falling over his forehead.

Jeff started back with Moose toward the Enlisted Mens' Club
where Moose was staying,
skirting firemen still hosing down the smoking ruins,
and police diverting traffic.
But before they got there, Jeff took a chance.
"Look, I've got a room. Why not stay over with me?"
"Sure," said Moose. "But you better watch out, lieutenant,
I'm not called Moose for nothing."
And he cupped his hands and made a moose call in the night.

Propped up against the pillows on the bed,

Jeff took covert looks
as Moose stripped down to his jockey shorts,
revealing his farm boy physique,
and Moose, noticing Jeff's admiration,
took a series of poses like in a body builder magazine.
"Come 'ere, Lieutenant, and feel this muscle," he said,
as he made his thigh muscles jump.
His blue eyes were clearly delighted with himself,
and he threw himself onto the bed,
kicking his legs in the air and whooping.

After the lights were turned out,
Jeff lay on his own side of the bed afraid to breathe,
longing for something to happen
but not knowing how to start.
It was Moose who said breathily, "Jesus, I'm hot.
Wouldn't me and Cherry have fun tonight."
And with a growl, he rolled onto Jeff
and wrestled him to an easy victory,
ending up sitting on his chest
and pinning his arms above him on the bed.
Then, Moose was lying on top of him,
his face nuzzling his neck,
saying, "This feels so good,
good as a woman,"
and Jeff felt the bulge in Moose's jockey shorts
hard against him.

The sex that was so casual and uncomplicated for the mechanic,
for Jeff was a bombshell.
The times before, when he'd had a guy's dick in his mouth,
and they'd shoved it down his throat,
he'd gagged and nearly strangled,
so after that he told guys he didn't do that kind of thing.
But this time it was different.
and Moose's cock moved with a rhythm
that let Jeff breathe—

each time he felt it throb it seemed to be speaking to him
and he let it slide down his open throat.
And after Moose came, in long spurts,
Jeff rested his head on the smooth belly
until Moose pulled him up and cradled him in his arms.
"Wow, you got a throat like a cunt," he said.

Then Moose wiped himself off with the edge of the sheet
and was asleep in a moment,
taking up most of the room with his arms and legs.
Jeff lay sleepless, his arm numb
under Moose's weight,
glancing in the darkness at the homely, innocent face
of the mechanic he had ended up in bed with.

The next morning, as they left the hotel,
Moose acted perfectly natural,
while Jeff was unable to talk much,
especially not about what had happened.
All he knew was that
nothing like this had ever happened to him before.

Back on the air base, there was no way
for an enlisted man and an officer
to hang around together,
so for Jeff it meant snatched moments:
He and Moose sometimes had their after-mission scotch
        together,
or Jeff would find excuses to go by the hangars,
where he might glimpse Moose up on a wing,
filling the fuel tanks,
and be rewarded by a sunny smile and wave of the hand.
Once in a while Jeff could get away with
going into the enlisted barracks to sit on Moose's bunk,
and listen to him talk cheerfully about home.

At the next officer's dance on base, while dancing together,

Pauline asked Jeff out of the blue,
"Luvvie, are you queer?"
"What do you mean?" Jeff said, flustered.
"Rita thinks so. I mean, it's all right with me, luv."
Jeff kept up the pretence, insisting
that he wasn't like that,
it was just that he was brought up to respect women,
and save it for marriage.
"Don't you know there's a war on?" Pauline snapped.
And Jeff was relieved when another officer cut in on them,
but still felt uncomfortable
when he saw her disappear with him
into one of the barracks.

After a series of missions
and with an overnight pass to London coming up,
Jeff asked Moose if they could get together again.
"I'll be going in with some of the guys," Moose said,
"so I don't know if I can make it,"
he flashed a smile at Jeff,
"but I'll try."

In London, Jeff didn't even go out to eat that night
but waited in his hotel room for hours,
until long after the pubs closed,
when a heavily-drunk Moose showed up.
This time, there was no hesitation,
and before undressing, Moose dived on top of Jeff
and hugged him in his arms.
The first time they'd done everything together
like two boys tumbling in the grass.
This time he pushed Jeff's head down.
"Okay, baby," he said, "suck it,
suck it like you mean it.
Let me feel you take it down,
down deep."
Jeff felt uncomfortable for a moment and resisted,

hen followed instructions—
ie was ready to accept whatever he could get.
And after Moose noisily came,
came beautifully,
he promptly passed out.
Undressing him, Jeff admired the smooth skin,
the not-too-muscled frame, the full genitals.
But in the morning, Moose said,
"Boy, was I drunk last night,"
as if he didn't remember a thing.

It drove Jeff crazy
that Moose wouldn't talk about them,
or acknowledge their special relationship.
The mechanic continued to treat him
as if they were just good buddies—
or officer and sergeant, with the respect
the ground crew had for the fly boys.
Without being too obvious,
Jeff kept trying to get Moose
to meet him again off base,
but he must have been pushing too hard,
because Moose started avoiding him.

Finally there was a showdown:
One night, Jeff was in the PX, talking
to Ralph of Special Services and Tony the Chaplain's assistant,
and covertly watching Moose across the room
where he was whooping it up with some buddies,
when he saw Moose leaving the PX alone.
He gave Ralph and Tony a quick excuse, and followed,
not noticing that they looked at each other with raised eyebrows.

It was especially dark out
with low clouds over the sky,
and every window covered for the blackout.
His heart beating, Jeff caught up with Moose,

132

determined to come straight out and ask
if Moose didn't feel something for him,
but the sergeant turned on him in the darkness
and blew up, complaining
that Jeff was making an asshole of himself.
"You got me all wrong, Lieutenant, y'hear?" he said, forcefully.
"I don't go that way, can't you understand?
I don't mind if you do,
but I don't."
And he loped off toward his barracks.

Jeff thought he was keeping his broken heart to himself,
but more experienced Ralph and Tony had spotted
Jeff's straying eyes in the PX
and understood his sudden exit.
The next time Ralph saw him,
he gave Jeff some advice—
that it was hopeless, and to get over it.
The only solution was to go out and get laid—a lot.
"Oh, you couldn't understand," Jeff said,
and walked off.

He had to talk to someone,
so on his next pass he didn't go to London,
but to the town near the base,
and waited for Pauline after she got through work
and asked her if she was free that night.
She was cool at first, but then gave in
when he told her how hard he was working.
She was going to a house party, she said,
if he wanted to come along.

The large villa on the edge of town,
owned by a local businessman,
was crowded with members of the Allied Forces,
and plenty of women both in uniform and civilian clothes.
There was a bartender making drinks, and a local dance band.

Jeff asked Pauline to dance,
intending to take her aside and come clean about himself,
but he was immediately cut in on.
He watched from the bar as she went from partner to partner,
and just when he thought they could be together for a while
and he'd get her off somewhere to talk,
traditional country dancing started, and all the Brits
lined up and went through the formal movements
they'd done all their lives.

Jeff, downing drink after drink at the bar,
heard someone say at his elbow,
"You ought to go out there and try it, mate."
A Brit in uniform, sandy-haired and sunburned,
was giving him a cheerful grin.
Jeff was about to snap back, "Why don't you?"
when he saw the cane.
"Got it in the leg in the desert," the young soldier said
as if reading his mind, "but it's just about healed.
I'd better give it a rest though, before I start leaping about.
Let's look for a more comfortable spot, hm?"
He gave Jeff a wink.
Jeff forgot about Pauline, as he and the limping soldier
wandered down a hallway opening doors,
looking into rooms where heavy breathing
alerted them to couples
squirming in the darkness.

They finally found an empty bedroom
with a bed piled with coats, and suddenly,
maybe it was the drinks or desperation or both,
Jeff pulled the soldier to him
and they fell together among the coats.
"Shut the door," the soldier said,
and their clothes were soon pulled apart.

Jeff was oblivious to everything

134

when the door opened
and a shaft of light from the hallway
fell across the two of them,
locked in each others' arms.
 "I was looking for you," a woman's voice said, "and ..."—
ending in a hiccup, as if she were drunk.
It was Pauline.
Jeff jumped up, pulling his clothes together,
as she gave a cry and staggered down the hall.
"I'm sorry," he said, as he followed her.
"I'm really sorry. Please understand, I...."
"I understand perfectly well, just leave me alone."
She was sobbing now.
"But I thought you knew ... you even said ...
Don't you remember you asked?"

They were out on the unlit street in the moonlight.
Pauline turned on him in hysterics.
"If you'd told me ... just told me ....
No, don't say anything.... I know.
Please go away,
go away and live your life...."
Following her as she staggered away,
Jeff tried to explain,
but she turned on him and yelled,
"It has nothing to do with me.
Just live your life, will you!
With whoever you want,
but live it!"
And when Jeff gave up and started back,
she yelled after him, "You bugger!
You dirty bugger!"

Jeff stayed in his bunk the following day,
pleading a hangover, but terrified
some of the guys might have heard the scene.
He was almost relieved to be flying again,

when he learned in the next morning's briefing
they were going to the industrial Ruhr again,
where the American losses were always high.

On the bombing run, dotted with blossoms of flak,
Jeff's plane had three of its engines shot out
and on the way home, with the gasoline
streaming from the wing tanks,
his pilot Chuck was forced to crash-land
on a temporary airstrip in France,
a hair-raising landing with only one engine
and the landing gear jammed.

Late that night, a truck arrived
to take Pete's crew to a regular airfield
where they could get a lift back to England.
But after they crowded onto the benches
in the back of the canvas covered truck,
another stranded crew piled in,
and Jeff found himself in the pitch blackness,
bumping along a rutted country road,
with a short and cuddly tail gunner on his lap.
Among snoozing soldiers in the truck's darkness,
the young gunner started breathing into Jeff's hair
and as if by accident his lips
grazed over Jeff's face and found his lips.

At an airbase in Normandy, while the downed crews
waited for a lift to England,
Jeff recklessly signed out a jeep from the motor pool
and drove with the gunner to the nearby coast,
stopped at a farmhouse
to buy cheese and bread and wine,
and rented a room in a French seaside hotel.
That night they wandered carelessly hand in hand
through the ghostly ruined harbor
and out on a dock where fishing boats were moored.

136

They were sitting in the stern of one of the boats
with their arms around each other
under a brilliant night sky,
when the fisherman came back.
"*Pas de problème,*" he said to them. "*Ne dérangez-vous pas,*"
and disappeared into the cabin.
A moment later, he looked out and pointed inside
to offer them a bunk,
but they refused, thanking him
in their high school French.

Jeff had taken a big chance going AWOL like that.
In his absence his crew
might have been flown back to England.
Luckily, when he returned to the base,
they were still waiting for a lift.
Chuck looked at Jeff quizzically
but asked no questions and Jeff didn't explain.
He just dived into bed, and only awakened for meals
and for the call that a plane had finally come
to take the crew home.

Ralph's advice had been right.
After this adventure,
Jeff wasn't hung up on Moose in the same way.
He'd catch sight of him with his buddies,
or working around the planes in his greasy coveralls—
he knew Moose's lanky body under the coveralls.
Those were heartstopping moments,
but when they passed each other
there was barely recognition on either side.

Through Ralph and his buddy Tony
Jeff began to meet other servicemen—
"that way" was the way you said it—
but felt uncomfortable on the base
or even in the nearby pub that they hung out in.

In the officer's club he was cruised by a ground officer,
who told him about The White Room,
a drinking club in London,
where he started going on his overnight passes.
It was no longer a question of furtive adventures.
On the advice of someone at the White Room bar,
he went to the theater and saw Gielgud in Hamlet,
Ivor Novello sing "*I'll gather lilacs in the spring again,*"
and a revue where a camp comedian, Hermione Gingold,
set her audience rocking with laughter.
A whole world was opening up to him.

On returning from London,
he heard that the pub off base, Tony and Ralph's hangout,
had been raided by the CID, the morals squad,
and Ralph had been caught
in one of the rooms upstairs with a paratrooper,
who swore to the agents that he was rough trade
and named other soldiers who "used his services,"
incriminating a number of GIs on the base.
Jeff felt sick.
It could happen to him too.
He could have been there, been picked up.

At the Officers' Club, Jeff's pilot, Chuck,
took him aside and warned him not to be so public
in his defense of Ralph.
Chuck said that he had been questioned by the CID
investigating the queer underground on the base.
"Don't worry, I covered for you," Chuck told him,
"but you could get into trouble."
Jeff was more shocked that Chuck knew about him all along,
than that he was under suspicion.
"It doesn't bother me," Chuck told him,
"but for God's sake, buddy, be careful."

In spite of Chuck's warning,

Jeff left a pub with a soldier,
after an exchange of significant looks,
and went into a bombed-out building for quick sex.
Afterwards, the soldier threatened him,
took his money and beat him up.
It was embarrassing around the crew with his facial bruises,
since he wasn't the type to get into brawls,
but Chuck made the whole thing a joke
and allayed suspicion.

Jeff was on tenterhooks about the continuing
investigation of gays on the base,
but as suddenly as it began
it was quashed as detrimental to the war effort.
Too late for Ralph, though,
who was sent back to the States
for discharge on a Section 8,
though Tony assured Jeff that it was no big deal,
Ralph would survive.

On the next bombing mission to Berlin,
Jeff's Flying Fortress was shot up bad
and limped back toward England on two engines.
Over the North Sea another engine gave out,
and flying low over the water,
one wing hanging down like a wounded bird,
the single engine coughed and died,
caught again and skipped over the water like a stone.
Preparing for the landing in the sea, the crew
crowded into the middle section of the plane
sitting on the floor, knees up against the man ahead.
They waited.
The engine stopped.
Then the plane crashed
into the water like a brick wall.

Jeff came to a moment later

with water rushing into the fuselage.
The crew was scrambling for the exit door on top,
pushing each other out.
They hauled themselves up one after another,
and jumped down onto the wing
where two rubber rafts
had automatically popped out of compartments
and inflated.

The whole crew got away before the plane sank,
but Chuck in the other raft
must have suffered internal injuries in the crash,
and after a while started gurgling yellow foam
and died.
Jeff and the crew bobbed for hours on the rough sea,
watching the returning aircraft overhead,
squadron after squadron,
too high up to notice the speck in the water below,
until they were spotted by an air-sea rescue cutter,
hauled up on deck by the British seamen,
and sent below to warm bunks with scratchy wool blankets,
except for poor Chuck's body on deck.

On their return to base, Jeff and his crew
were treated as heroes, everybody wanted to hear the story,
and for the first time in weeks
Moose made friendly overtures to Jeff.
"You really had us worried, Lieutenant," he said.
But Pauline's friend Rita, who had been hoping
to go back to the States
as Chuck's war bride,
was devastated
when Jeff called
and told her of his death.

At the next base dance, Pauline kissed Jeff on the cheek
and said, "Is everything all right, luv?"

"Yes," he answered, choking up
for the first time after the crash.
Holding his hand, she asked him to forgive her
for the scene that night of the party—
she was pissed.
He had a right to live any way he wanted,
especially with him risking his life
every day in the war.
Tears ran down Jeff's cheeks that she understood.
Then in the highest spirits he had ever seen her,
she danced the whole evening
with one Yank after another,
and when she sashayed out boldly to the barracks
on the arm of the squadron leader, a captain,
she winked at Jeff,
and he felt as if a burden were lifted.

On VE Day, there was no celebration
for Jeff and his buddies.
While the British went wild all over the country,
the Americans, unaccountably, were confined to base—
a chickenshit decision of the top brass.
But the following week, the flying crews
flew the ground crews over the Ruhr
to see the ruins of the German cities they had helped destroy.
In the nose of Jeff's B-17, Moose watched
as they circled the Cologne Cathedral,
pocked with holes, but with its two lacy spires still standing.
On landing, the new pilot, Chuck's replacement,
took a picture of them together in front of the plane,
each with an arm around the other,
and joked about "you two lovebirds."

The next week, Jeff got his orders—
he was being redeployed to the States,
for training in B-29s,
the longer range bombers needed in the Pacific

to strike Japan.
With nothing to lose
he asked the mechanic to meet him in London.
The fantasies of forever Jeff had had
were gone,
and they spent the night like good buddies.
Again, Moose said with a grin,
"Lieutenant, that throat of yours is like a cunt.
I'm gonna miss it."
And he gave his rebel yell.
"I bet you will, you horny bastard," said Jeff,
mussing up with his hand the sandy hair
that fell over Moose's forehead,
and added, "I'll miss you, too."
That was as far as he could go.
By now, he knew better than to say more,
or to expect anything more—they were good buddies
and it was okay.
He was able to listen, over the hotel breakfast,
their last breakfast,
to Moose going on
about how much he was looking forward
to seeing Cherry and his family in Oklahoma.
After Moose returned to the base,
Jeff stayed on in London and went to his club, the White Room,
where his drinking companions at the bar
gave him addresses in New York
of restaurants and bars, people to look up.

Jeff never was deployed to the Pacific, after all,
for the war there ended, too,
and after he was discharged in the fall,
a card came from Moose that he was home
with his wife and family.
Jeff smiled at the childish scrawl.

૨૭

After the fiftieth anniversary celebration—
with Vera Lynn singing "We'll Meet Again"
and a troupe of dancers doing a poor imitation of
      jitterbugging—
Jeff returns to his hotel and sits on the bed,
looking at the photo of Moose and himself together,
the one taken the day they flew around the Cologne Cathedral.
"Lovebirds," the pilot called them.
It was an affair which could only have happened
in the dislocations of wartime.
They were from different worlds,
and without the war would never have met.
But out of that dark time, that unreality,
his real life began.

THE POETRY FILE

THE POETRY FILE

> With a talent for speech,
> I had no language.

Poetry for me, as for many American poets, is a rescue from incoherence. We don't have the language in our bones. We are pre-literate.

I write in the language inside my head, the language I think in, but then, oddly, it gets judged by the language, and standards, of the outside world. Like my dreams of being naked among the clothed, my poems expose me to the world. Maybe it's one of the reasons I write, but I envy poets who keep buttoned up.

Today, you are almost made to feel you don't have a right to be a poet if you are not reticent.

Without any Jewish education, still, fragments of talmudic thinking, cabbalistic anti-logic, Yiddish insight, inform my literary method and judgments. Though I rarely use religious symbolism and themes, I'm a very Jewish poet, in the secular socialist Enlightenment tradition.

> I have one language inside my head
> but speak a different language outside,

> like my parents who spoke Yiddish together,
> and English to us,
> except in my case,
> both languages, inside and outside,
> are English
> and only in poetry do they blend.

I don't speak Yiddish, but in my poetry I try to leave in any Yiddish word order or turn of phrase or intonation surviving from childhood. Locked into them are layers of old feeling, some of which I am barely in touch with and have to discover.

> The reason I need to write poetry is
> I keep forgetting important things
>
> like my feelings.

I use a local New York syntax, a kind of Jewish syntax that New Yorkers use in everyday life. Howard Moss, the *New Yorker*'s poetry editor, rejected my poem "New York" on the grounds that the first line was ungrammatical, which might be true, but it sounded like the way I'd say it.

> I live in a beautiful place, a city
> people claim to be astonished
> when you say you live there….

The irony was that he later included the poem in his anthology of poems about New York.

"The art, *mes enfants*, is to be completely yourself," Paul Verlaine has been quoted as saying. But some writers see being a writer as putting on an act. Still, what's wrong with re-inventing yourself?

Without undervaluing elaborate syntax and elegant language, I prefer to explore the poetry of everyday expression. I'm not alone in this. Poets all over the country are doing it. Long Beach poet Gerald Locklin describes it as "the movement towards the spoken idiom."

148

Poetry-as-Language vs. Poetry-as-Voice. Or poetry for the voice.

Strange how hard it is to avoid archaic/poetic language. I started a poem "It behooves us to…" Where in hell did that come from?

Why do I write the way I do? Much of my life has been spent in a state of fear and confusion. Clarity, therefore, has been my goal. My poems are moments of hard-won clarity. Therefore, obscurity, one of the pillars of Modern Poetry, makes no sense for me.

For Modern Poetry, obscurity was always a rallying cry. Telling straight out what was going on or what you meant was relegated to the lesser realm of journalism, or perhaps fiction, which catered to lower tastes. Poetry, Modern Poetry, was oblique and floated in a haze of ambiguity and allusion, rejecting any reader except the most highbrow, with whom you were in complicity to make it difficult. But the main thing for me is that I've always wanted my poetry to be understood by anybody. Unfortunately, if editors can easily understand what you are saying, they figure it's no good as poetry.

I don't see why poetry can't be as readable as prose. In fact, it seems to me that poetry should be easier to read than prose. A poem is short, usually, and the lines are broken up into nice little segments that clarify the ideas. I make it even easier with my narrative style.

It is still repeated as dogma that "subject matter" is not what poetry is about—the put-down word is "referential"—and that everything has already been said in poetry. But why limit the possibilities? The whole point of poetry for me is subject matter, saying what I have to say, saying what's never been said before, what's not polite to say.

"A verbal art like poetry is reflective; it stops to think." W. H. Auden.

There's always been too much description in poetry for my tastes. Trying to describe something in words that could better be shown in a picture is boring. But why shouldn't poetry talk about interesting things, tell good stories, discuss controversial issues? That's where I've gotten into trouble. My poetry is "referential."

≈

One of my poems, "The Romance of Extinct Birds: The Carrier Pigeon," was accepted by *The Atlantic Monthly* with the condition that I drop from the title the word "Extinct," on the grounds that carrier pigeons were not extinct. During the first of many phone conversations with the editor I argued weakly that it had been my boyhood belief that they had become extinct, and that's why the poem was called "The *Romance* of Extinct Birds." I got no editorial sympathy for that argument and was told the facts in poems must be correct. So, of course, I had to agree to the change if I wanted to be published by them. The title would therefore be "The Carrier Pigeon."

Then I got a letter from the editor, worrying about my use of the word "screwing" in the line, "They weren't like most pigeons/for whom corn and screwing make up the good life," on the grounds that pigeons do not screw. I answered that I'd seen the males hopping onto the backs of the ladies and *shtupping* away, much as humans do. We had further telephone discussions in which the editor declared that he observed pigeons on the Boston Common all the time, and they did not do anything like screwing, while I kept insisting that male and female pigeons had little genitals like ours. I started to wonder if, in the respectable world that *Atlantic Monthly* readers and editors lived in, far from my grubby New York precincts, he might be right.

I was finally informed that ornithologists had been consulted and I was wrong. But even so, I was not willing to substitute the saccharine "corn and cooing" for "corn and screwing," and said I was willing to change the word to "copulation" perhaps. Then, the page proof came and I corrected the typos and returned it, so I figured, even if the poem was looking more and

150

more strange to me, I was home free, and looked forward, at least, to my check.

However, after several months, I received another letter saying the editors still found it unacceptable for the poem in its text to claim that carrier pigeons had become extinct, though I continued to argue that in my boyhood memory, at least, they disappeared from the face of the globe, and that the poem was about memory, nostalgia, loss, and heroism. But again I was told sternly that the facts in poetry must be correct, with the implication that it was people like me who give poetry the bad reputation of being airy-fairy, and if I expected them to publish my poem, I had to rewrite it. But in continuing discussions over the phone—this went on for months—my editor suddenly shouted that he was sick of the whole thing and to forget it.

I was delighted when, a short while later, the more liberal *Nation* magazine accepted the poem, and published it as I wanted. Irrelevant as it is for my poem, it seems that pigeons actually don't have little penises and vaginas, but some other apparatus. But I would say the crucial problem was that I used the word "screw," and the dignified *Atlantic Monthly* could not put it in print—though they would never admit that to me, and had to find all kinds of other excuses to drop the poem.

I had a similar problem with a poem accepted by the *New Yorker*, "My Sister, the Queen," which explores the sad life of Princess Margaret. After the poem was kept on ice for several years, it was finally scheduled for the issue of March 10, 1997, when I got a call from the fact checker, who disputed my version of what happened to the young princess when she wanted to marry the divorced commoner Group Capt. Peter Townsend. The fact checker said that according to her source, a book about the royals, it was not the Queen who had prevented Margaret from marrying Townsend, but the British Cabinet. Naturally, I told her, that was the official version. They would never attribute such an unpopular decision to the Sovereign. The fact checker, who was, of course, too young to have been around when it all happened, asked for proof. Proof? I told her that the version in my poem is what everyone knew to be true at the time. I argued,

151

as I did with the *Atlantic Monthly,* that in any case I was dealing with the myth of the past, which was more important than the official records. But this did not get to her either. Here, too, I was asked to rewrite the poem to conform to the "facts," and when I refused, it was dropped from the issue.

It is likely that the *New Yorker* editor Tina Brown, a Brit, bumped the poem herself, and simply assigned the fact checker the dirty work of dealing with me. In fact, when I asked the fact checker to consult her editor about my version of the Margaret story, she said, revealingly, "She's already seen it." An English friend I told the story to understood at once that Tina Brown did not want to offend the Palace in any way because she eventually hoped for royal honors, to be damed.

It's a small consolation that everybody agrees the poetry in the *New Yorker* is generally awful, and hardly anybody bothers to read it.

Almost every poem I write seems to have in it something that makes it unpublishable. I always thought that's what good writing was all about, saying what's unacceptable, shocking the respectable world. That's just my unreconstructed bohemianism. I still believe that one of the wonderful things about poetry is that you are free to tell your secrets, even supposed to tell your secrets. Though when I write, I never remember that it's going to be embarrassing to read in public.

My poetry has also been criticized as being "just" therapy. It's too personal, too psychological. But I was in therapy of one kind or another for years, and it naturally was reflected in my poetry.

When the "confessional" school of poetry emerged, formalist poets like Robert Lowell tried to loosen up and let down their hair. But the thing about their so-called "confessional" poetry was that it didn't ever really spill the beans. My poetry denies that there is anything too intimate to be written about. Very different from the "confessional" poets, with their emotional outpourings embalmed in a high-literary manner.

152

Exercises for writing workshop: Write poem to the parent you have the most difficulty with and say to them what you've always wanted to say. Tell a secret you've never told anyone. (But students often can't do this, because they don't want the other students to hear, to know what they're really like.)

‿

From an Introduction to a new edition of *Stand Up, Friend, With Me*

When I started writing poetry in the late forties, if you wanted to be part of Modern Poetry—and I did, desperately—narrative or explanatory material was to be deleted in the long process of revision—T. S. Eliot's "The Waste Land" was the paradigm. It was the rule to leave your personal life out of the poem as much as possible. No bitching, and there was no question of mentioning your aches and pains or your lower regions. Perhaps this was a reaction to Victorian poets rhapsodizing over their sensibilities, but continued their puritanism. Language had to be austere.

You were also supposed to be above reading your poems well. That would have been interpreted as catering to the audience. Top poets like Wallace Stevens and Auden mumbled their poems. In other words, it was to be made clear to the audience that this wasn't show business but Serious Business. This was before Dylan Thomas came to the U.S. and made readings a performance (his excuse being that he was Welsh)—though Frost, too, had always been a magnificent reader of his work. Still, Frost was looked down on somewhat, and his straightforward narrative poems made "us moderns" uncomfortable. But the incorporation of a colloquial voice into his formal verse was extraordinary for the time.

Dylan Thomas soon had American poets declaiming their poetry, though mostly in the elevated tones of preachers, again reminding the listener that poetry was a spiritual exercise, and not entertainment. It must also have been Dylan Thomas who in the postwar decade unloosed the Beats' rhapsodic, so-called

153

bardic style, which was outrageously theatrical. But it was as if the personal voice, the speaking voice, or indeed the daily concerns that we all live and suffer over, had no place in poetry. Unfortunately, with a few exceptions, poetry at most poetry readings still is mostly incomprehensible, and therefore its main attraction is the novelty of getting to look at the poet.

Poetry, back then, was divided into "serious" and "light" verse and there was no intercourse between the two, though the first breakthrough came when Oscar Williams included a section of light verse in his landmark anthology of modern poetry after WWII. Still, W. H. Auden was often funny, witty, sly, or campy in his poetry, and I took courage from that, though publishing anything with humor was not so easy in those days. God, editors were conservative and stuffy! But it's almost as bad nowadays.

Sex was another taboo. The words in your head, the words that you actually thought in, must not appear in print. You didn't dare put a four-letter word into a poem, or write about half the stuff one really worries about in life, even when it finally became okay to do it in prose. Somebody did once sneak the word "gloryhole" into a poem in the *New Yorker* past the watchdog eyes of the editors, but the content of the magazine never recognized the fact that a large proportion of its readers has always been gay.

That leads back to the question of subject matter, and modern poetry does not deal with "subject matter." Editors will enforce that edict. Not just your sexlife was out, but politics, health problems, race problems—in fact, almost anything I wanted to write about. And if it was funny or satirical, that made it light verse, and therefore not Poetry.

The worst thing about Modern Poetry for me, and what made me so uncomfortable, was that it was cold—even when passionate it was cold and hard. Yet my poetry was warm and soft. This was attacked as sentimental, a charge that is leveled at any display of feelings. The poetry establishment, especially in writing workshops, has perpetrated one of the worst evils, to my mind, in making a distinction between sentiment and sentimentality, which is parroted like dogma, but which I see as a straightjacket young poets are put into by their teachers. What's wrong

154

with feeling in poetry, for God's sake? But then it might be taken for sentimentality. The result has been that a straightforward expression of honest feeling is rare.

By persistence, I did get a lot of poems, eventually, into literary magazines, but my manuscript got twenty-four rejections before winning the Lamont Award, making its publication possible. And by the time it was published in 1963, much had changed in the poetry world and it was generally praised even for those qualities that had made it so difficult to find a publisher.

❧

Letter to the *NY Times* (never sent)

I want to register my protest at the way the *Book Review* presents poetry as the dreariest of academic disciplines, an exercise in language, making it so conventional and safe that no one could possibly care about it.

I never wanted to write poetry that sounded like poetry. And I still don't want the language of my poems to be noticeable or distracting, so that the poem can talk straight to the heart and the mind. But the critics, fashionably, concentrate on language. Even the editors are first looking for language (fancy, self-conscious, odd, willed), language that stands out, or it's not poetry for them. My language is criticized as cliché because it's based on the way I talk. But Auden and Cavafy were both plainspoken poets.

> I'm suspicious of fancy language.
> I always imagine the most elegant poets
> have shitty toilets, dirty asses.
> In their lives they're dirty,
> and like everyone, do dirty things.
>
> Even Stevens, too pure ever to use the words,
> I like to think of holding his cock
> and farting with gusto.

After hearing Elizabeth Bishop's memoir of Marianne Moore on the radio

What was wrong with modern poetry back then was that it was in the hands of prudes/stuffed shirts like Marianne Moore and T. S. Eliot. And what about Marianne's father, Mr. Moore? There wasn't a mention of him. He may have been a rat, maybe skipped out, but I couldn't help feeling sorry for him living with Marianne and her mother.

A pity that Bette Davis didn't record the poetry of Marianne Moore. With her verbal mannerisms, quirky rhythm, she would have been perfect.

Poetry is not far from my everyday thoughts and emotions, so writing it can be as uncomplicated as making a note to myself. The trouble is that when the words or a line come into my head, maybe while I'm shaving or lying in bed, they seem so obvious that it hardly seems worth the bother of putting them down, and I have to remember and force myself to jot them into my notebook. But when I look at them later, they're not ordinary at all.

The great leap   over the gap
between getting an idea   and writing it down

nothing special, you think   or
no reason to write that down   I'll remember it, it's so obvious

and the surprise later   when I look at it again.

For me, poetry aims for the simplest possible language. Prose needs florid passages for variety, effect. Continual simple language in prose is monotonous. On the other hand, I always liked the dictum (by whom?) that poetry should be at least as well-written as prose.

I try to say what I have to say in a minimum of words, the words that say it perfectly, which is my definition, not of poetry, but of poetic language.

156

"No poet worth his salt is going to be handsome if he or she is beautiful." John Berryman.

Actually, we used to fantasize about the beauties among the poets—Frederick Prokosch, W. S. Merwin—whose blurry snapshots were included in the Oscar Williams' anthology. But in that severe era dominated by the New Criticism and the puritanism of T. S. Eliot, the poet's beauty was not to be taken into consideration in reading the poetry.

Today, being good-looking in our age of hype is no longer considered dubious, but an asset.

⁊❧

SECRETS OF THE CLOSET

Rupert Brooke was one of my earliest poetic loves, as much for his legend as his poetry. As with so many poets, the legend lent his poetry an extra dimension. He was such a famous beauty he expected every man to make love to him, but I heard that when he met Henry James, poor James, though smitten, had to stammer through his famous excuse about an accident, reported variously as stepping over a stile or stumbling off a streetcar, which left him incapable.

On picnics, Rupert Brooke displayed an unusual talent—after jumping into an ice-cold pond, he emerged, not shrivelled up like us normal men, but with a hard-on, which he displayed proudly to the girls and boys of the party. Not the usual Victorian scene.

Modern poetry was supposed to be a rebellion against the "poetical" language of Victorian sensibilities, but gentility keeps creeping back in. It's the curse of poetry. That's why I like to publish in little magazines like *Exquisite Corpse* and *Chiron Review* and *5AM*, where they are open to the new low-down, vernacular poetry, and everything is allowed. I did have a poem about my cock in an academic quarterly, the *Michigan Quarterly Review* (I praise the editor, Laurence Goldstein for this)—the subject of the issue was

The Male Body. But there are still plenty of restrictions in this country.

John Crowe Ransom, editor of *Kenyon Review*, to Robert Duncan, 12/6/44, rejecting a poem. "I read the poem as an advertisement or a notice of overt homosexuality, and we are not in the market for literature of this type."

In the early sixties, one of Alfred Chester's stories was also rejected by *Partisan Review* on the grounds that it "celebrated homosexuality instead of being analytical about it." Even today, plenty of censorship exists. What's so terrible about the word "hard-on," for instance? But try to get a poem published with that word in it.

It often depends on the political views of the editor. The Boston gay paper, *Bay Windows*, not long ago refused to print a poem of mine because I used the word "queer," which was unacceptable to the editor.

Back in the 40s and 50s, homosexuality was okay in poetry if it was veiled by metaphor, ambiguous pronouns, and verbal brilliance. I was a passionate admirer of the poetry of Dunstan Thompson, with its unmistakable homoerotic content. But after Senator Joseph McCarthy and HUAC got done with the universities and intellectuals and made them knuckle under, poetry was not considered a medium for anything more than spiritual subject matter—nuns, swans, carousels, etc. Or philosophizing. Academic and establishment poetry was reinforced in its gentility. Then the Beats came along, a breath of fresh air. But essentially they didn't change the poetry world, which is a very conservative establishment.

With its dedication to ambiguity, Modern Poetry fit right in with the need of gay poets to be closeted. Poets in the past have often changed the sex of the lover addressed—Byron's love poems to Lord Clare, for example, to the feminine pseudonym of "Thyrza." Of course, one can always address the lover with the anonymous "you" and it can be taken by the reader according to his own sexual preference. Hart Crane, openly gay in his life, in his work was cautious. But one can learn to read through the veils of metaphor.

Even straight poets found the devices of Modern Poetry useful. Henri Coulette was obsessed in his poetry with the secret world of spies, agents, traitors. "War of the Secret Agents," a marvelous sequence of poems about spies in occupied Paris, seemed to be his metaphor for human relations, where nobody knows the truth of anybody else and what secrets are hidden, with betrayal a constant. Was life under an oppressive occupying army also a metaphor for his own secret life, the betrayal he himself might have been forced to commit? His mysterious poem "Chicken Rampant, Bar Sinister," suggests an adolescent hustler phase, a court case where he had to testify against one of his johns, a spell with a psychiatrist.

CHICKEN RAMPANT, BAR SINISTER

I tell him my thirteen secret names,
and I say,
"All my decisions are committee decisions,
and some of my selves,
Doctor, are always out of town."
Rich as Onassis, I count my fears.
In my dreams
I see the hard-hearted and familiar strangers
circling around me,
and I don't know if I'm their king

or their victim. Chicken rampant, bar
sinister—
my family coat of arms hangs, invisible,
in an empty room.
Memory's a form of simile:

I am like all my unknown and frightened fathers.

Surely, I am not making up the plot I discern through the fragmentary technique, a teenage boy caught hustling in a gay bar, and sent to a psychiatrist by the family, thereby being frightened into conformity.

When I stopped over in L.A. on a reading tour, Coulette came to interview me for a book of interviews of poets. He was dressed academic conservative-style, with horn-rimmed glasses, appropriate to a professor at the U. of Southern California, not in the least California-casual, even slightly stuffy in manner. He gave nothing away, if there was anything to give away.

I've written to his friend, Donald Justice, to ask if he knew anything about Coulette's early life, but he didn't—Coulette was a very private man. But perhaps I am reading into this poem what I want to find there? In the other poems I can find no other references to a gay past or a double life, and even in "Chicken Rampant, Bar Sinister" it takes close reading to dig out the story, and what one gets is merely tantalizing.

⁊ʊ

Helen Vendler writes approvingly of: "The visible estrangement of poetry from prose." Odd that critics should try to make rules for poets.

Actually, poetry and prose draw closer together on the West Coast, draw further apart on the East Coast, where poetry becomes more literary, moves toward artifice.

When poetry is talked about by critics like Vendler, I rarely recognize myself.

> I'm the Eileen Farrell of the poetry world.
> A glorious voice, but low class,
> living with her policeman husband
> on Staten Island,
>
> Staten Island, for God's sake,
> prole heaven—
>
> and far too low class for the Met.

160

The problem I've had from the beginning was that I wrote for people like myself, assuming they were out there, but the poetry world says, You must write for Us.

I see poetry as a *vehicle*, but there are many different possibilities: Ashbery, for instance, writes in the *manner* of someone writing a poem. It is an act that sometimes breaks down into giggles. With the Beats, the *impulse* to write poetry was demonstrated, emphasizing verbal improvisations. Now Helen Vendler, as premier critic, celebrates the *means* of poetry: language, form, diction, metaphor. I think she misses what poetry is really about.

> Mannerisms
> do not make it poetry,
> but sometimes they succeed.

Charles Reznikoff on the difference between formal and free verse:

> "Not like flowers in the city
> in neat rows or in circles
> but like dandelions
> scattered on a lawn."

Maybe what it comes down to is, Do you like the sensibility?

HOLY MEN, ALL

> Rilke in religious mode
> minimized our mortal ills.
> Wordsworth in his greatest ode
> chortled over daffodils,
> In Dylan Thomas' poetry
> Christmas was holy in his town.
> Poets always claim to be
> enlightened, God-struck, never down.
> I try, I try, but this morning I
> only see God in a stream of shit—
> alas, again denied me. Why?
> And why scorn my laments for it?

If poets fill their poems with praise
of angels, mystic visions, flowers,
Field sings of constipated days
wasted on toilet seat for hours.
Such honest songs will never win
a MacArthur prize, and even worse,
the critics will never let him in-
to *The Oxford Book of Modern Verse.*

ॐ

SECRETS OF THE CLOSET

Whatever Harold Norse says in his memoirs about the meeting of Chester Kallman and W. H. Auden, the version I heard from Robert Friend was that when Auden and Isherwood came to this country and gave a reading, Brooklyn College students Kallman and Norse decided to go after the great men. Norse and Isherwood, after a one-night stand, didn't hit it off, but Kallman landed Auden and it stuck, with historic results.

In 1946, when I was a student, I went to hear Dunstan Thompson at the Poetry Center. Afterwards, Norse started chatting with me in the lobby and joined me on the subway downtown. As a neophyte, I was flattered that he would bother to talk poetry with me. When we arrived at Penn Station and I said goodbye, I had to catch my train home to Long Island where I lived with my parents, he said crossly, What did I waste my time with you for? And jumped on the subway back to the Y to pick somebody else up.

I was something of a cockteaser back then. I wanted to be wanted, but didn't want to have to go through with it, especially with Harold Norse!

SORRY, I NEVER SLEPT WITH ALLEN GINSBERG

What poet does not rejoice
at the death of a poet—
like the young princess,
who studied the line of succession.

162

"I see that I am closer to the throne
than I had thought," she said.
Still a child, it was in her blood
to consider doing
a Richard the Third herself
to clear her path.
Even I, taking up as little space as possible,
am blocking others,
the hungry, the unpublished,
behind me, saying,
"Get the hell out of my way."

Allen Ginsberg took up a lot of space.
Relieved now at his absence,
we are all the more eager
to praise him into stone,
embalm him in sainthood.
The only trouble is
that in death as in life
he is protean—
he spreads everywhere now.
Our country has an immense
debt of gratitude to him,
for it was his lone voice,
half-crazy but unmistakable,
that announced the end
of the reign of terror in the Fifties,
an Age of Injustice,

when they actually got almost everybody
to believe that this country
was about to be taken over
by a handful of lefties,

when free thought
was made a crime,
with black lists, imprisonment, and executions—

the mad doctor, Wilhelm Reich, dying in jail,

his books and orgone boxes burned,
because he preached good sex as a cure,

the Rosenbergs
fried in the electric chair
for being communists,

homosexuals declared dangerous
to national security,
hunted down and fired from their jobs,
even lobotomized,

university teachers
forced to sign loyalty oaths,

writers, actors, and directors sent to jail,
denied passports,
forbidden to work,

and the great Paul Robeson
ruined—
when the entire creative world of the left
turned against itself,
proving their patriotism
in denouncing each other.

How gloomy was the Village in those years,
the San Remo bar nearly deserted,
with everyone going to their analysts—
as if we could cure the world on the couch.

Then came "Howl,"
a cry of defiance,
declaring the right to be whatever we are,
a mere poem that destroyed the destroyers,
the haters,
the killers in our government
and gave courage to the oppressed.
Everything started coming alive again.
The courts allowed banned books

to be published,
Mayor Lindsay stopped the police
from raiding gay bars,
and liberation was in the air.
Though nothing could heal the damage done
from the fear of ideas, of intelligence,
implanted by the witch hunters
in the national psyche—

a permanent trauma
that only one Allen Ginsberg
couldn't heal.
Though he tried.

This uncircumcized Jew,
with his Old Testament voice,
in the best Jewish tradition
was completely down to earth,
a mensch.
When he gave a reading in Miami Beach
at my sister's neighborhood temple,
she called out over the crush of
adoring matrons around him,
"Allen, my brother is Edward Field,"
and he answered with the gentlest of mockery,
"Hello, Edward Field's Miami Beach sister."
He even reduced top poetry critic Helen Vendler,
who had to detest his messy poems,
to coy, shivering approval—
though that was more the Politics of Power
rather than any yielding to the genuine.

Throughout the cold war
he remained faithful
to his communist mother,
though his own communism was not
the rigid, puritanical variety
but a kind that has room for all of us,

that wants us to be ourselves.
He belonged to a bohemian left
the witch hunters
could never understand
when they put artists and thinkers in jail—
a left which included
sex and astrology,
buddhist chanting and modern dance
and marijuana.
If it's real communism
it should let everybody live.

I hardly knew Allen Ginsberg,
but since we're from the same generation and queer,
I'm always asked by the young
if I ever went to bed with him.
Since he's no longer around to deny it,
I think I'll start saying I did,
though I'm pretty sure we weren't each other's type.
I don't think he'd mind.
He liked saying, "I've had him,"
about everybody famous,
or just anybody—he took sex as a right.
Gary Lenhart once reported
after getting in the sack with him
that Ginsberg made love
"in a friendly fashion."

The rich and famous,
like Jacqueline Kennedy Onassis,
don't have to die in agony.
It's pretty clear
that after the fatal diagnosis
his death, like hers,
was helped along.
All over the country there is agreement,
if it's hopeless,
why not help end the suffering

before it becomes unbearable?
But the government won't listen.
Still, nobody objects
that in AIDS, at the unbearable stage,
you will be given morphine drip,
if the family approves.

Even our most famous poet,
world famous,
you don't expect the Nobel Prize
if you shoot your mouth off like he did.
But surely Poet Laureate?
No, even there—too queer, too radical.
The government would rather play it safe
with tame, academic poets
who keep their mouths shut
about injustice—
all of them, to date,
straight.
On his death
his government didn't honor him
as any civilized country would have.
There were no mass funeral processions,
the President made no official eulogy
about the loss to the nation,
proclaimed no moment of silence.
There was no resting place
for his ashes
in a pantheon of the great.

He didn't need any of that.
When he died,
the earth shook.

ɞ

"Everything that comes within the Modernist movement employs modes of discourse and sequences of images that are oblique; such poetry is on the whole inaccessible to many readers

167

and perhaps to all readers unprovided with some kind of commentary." J. M. Cameron (*NY Review of Books*)

This is the academic view of what happened in the great modernist revolution early this century. It's true that the new poetry rejected the debased popular culture the poets fled from. But they were also reacting against the stilted literary language of Victorian and Edwardian poetry. Technique became more self-conscious, which meant greater demands on the poet, as well as greater demands on the reader's attention, which had the effect of losing whatever readership there had been for poetry in the nineteenth century. They just couldn't understand it anymore.

But the struggle for poetry goes back and forth. Some see the divergence toward the high falutin' as having been engineered by T. S. Eliot, until the Beats brought it back again, via William Carlos Williams, to its original radical impulse. At the moment the literary establishment is promoting a more literary, self-conscious language, and the Beats seem to have failed, though out there across the country poetry looks a very different thing than from New York and the élite universities of the Northeast.

Maybe it was natural that the reaction of modern poets against the sentimentality of popular culture, commercialism, the debased language of newspapers, should have resulted in a super-aesthetic stance, as if being difficult to understand would separate one from the mob. But being afraid of vulgarity often leads to just another form of gentility. The trap many poets fall into. That's why I talk about shitting in my poetry. I'm just another person who wipes his ass.

I'm proud not to be a holier-than-thou academic. In a way, I have no literary pretensions.

> Poetry is no big deal.
> It is what it is natural to speak
> if you are connected to your feelings.

168

In England at a friend's house, unable to sleep, I turned to the bedside books, and tried to read from a volume of Keats. It was startling that only the famous poems were successful, and in fact stood out like diamonds in a mass of sludge.

Could it have been the opium-based medications that opened him up for his great moments?

Then I tried *The Oxford Book of English Verse*. Mostly unreadable, except for the masterpieces.

I remembered how puzzled I was at the beginning, trying to read poetry, fascinated but bored. So what my own poetry set out to do was *not* sound like that, make poetry interesting for people like me.

The big question: Why is it so boring? Of course, certain poems are thrilling, but the rest are boring.

> I read it dutifully, until
> rarely,
> something happens.

Poetry for me is saying interesting things—interesting and inspiring things, that in the saying, help people, point to a better life.

> Writing it
> is much better than reading it.
> Maybe poetry is only fun
> if you write it.

My favorite poem is the 23rd Psalm, which I see as a useful one. It is healing. Every line makes me think. I say it over and over in the night.

I have a gut feeling that poetry should heal.

Title for Arab/Jewish poetry anthology:
SO WE SHOULDN'T KILL EACH OTHER.

Sex and religion come together in the poetry of K'bir, a terrific combination, marvelous to read when stoned.

"Relentlessly high-minded"—a phrase no longer heard, but applies to Helen Vendler, Harold Bloom, Susan Sontag, and the like. They revel in literary affectation, but it could also be seen as an advanced form of play, so who could condemn it?

Poetry is not (just) fancy language—this is a common mistake.

> If it looks like a poem
> > you read it differently,
> > > even when the words are prosaic.

> It is not "serious,"
> > it is playfulness,
> > > it is play.

Sometimes serious play: Like Stanley Moss whose composition method reminds me of Hans Christian Andersen's little boy captured by the Ice Queen playing endlessly with alphabet blocks of ice. He will call me up with one new version of a poem after another, and I recognize discarded lines from years before. Chunks of it disappear but will turn up in a later poem.

☙

I was in an Indian restaurant in the Village having lunch with friends when an elderly man with a grizzled beard came in and, while waiting for someone, kept restlessly walking up and down the aisle. You couldn't miss him, he was wearing a fire-red duffel coat, though the room was warm. A friend at my table asked what I thought about John Ashbery, and as the man in the red coat passed by us he bent over and said, "Be careful what you say. Ashbery is Harold Bloom's favorite poet." I could only think of the lame reply, "But Bloom's in New Haven." "He also teaches at NYU now," the man said.

During the rest of the meal, Bloom (for the man had to be

him), still in his fiery coat, sat at a nearby table, presenting his profile to the restaurant. I kept thinking of what I might have said to him. Join us for a drink, at least? Missed opportunity.

ஓ

SECRETS OF THE CLOSET

The sexuality of the British is a mystery to me. Poets like Stephen Spender and George Barker were gay, yet had several wives. I once wildly admired Barker's book-length narrative poem *Noctambules* that went, "The gay paraders of the esplanade, the wanderers in time's shade...."

A friend who knew Spender at the Gargoyle Club, the literary hangout in London during the war, said Spender claimed to have made love with GIs from every state, but preferred farm boys from Ohio.

During the war in London, a man at a bar recited to me what he claimed was an early love lyric of Spender's, that Spender had given him. I don't believe it is in his *Collected* and could have been lost or suppressed:

> You and I were playing
> when suddenly I
> wanted more than play with you.
>
> (missing stanza)
>
> Blinded by my will
> it took me time to find
> that you were playing still.

How hypocritical of Spender to bring a lawsuit against David Leavitt over his novel, even if it was based on episodes from his autobiography. The sex scenes certainly were graphic, but marvelous, and the book was not offensive in any way—besides it was fiction. But canny Spender, the lawsuit rekindled his faded career and his work came back into print for a final burst of glory before he died.

"I Think Continually of Those Who Were Truly Great" was always one of my favorite poems, and I can still remember most of it. But Spender lost his class for me when he was revealed to have accepted CIA money for his magazine *Encounter*, making it an instrument of the cold war.

When I was living in Paris in 1948, on a visit to London over Christmas I phoned Spender, asking if I could meet him. He invited me to his house and we had tea in his study. His hand was on my knee in no time, but even if I had been attracted to him—and he was a tall, strikingly handsome man—I could hear his wife, children, and the household staff just beyond the door!

Later he took me to a cocktail party at the Gargoyle Club, given by Rose Macaulay, where, dazzled, I met numerous literary people I had only heard about before. When T. S. Eliot arrived, pushing his roommate Max Hayward's wheelchair into the room, a young novelist I was standing with kept saying, "Let's introduce the two Americans." I would have died of embarrassment.

I had a lot of dark curly hair and an olive complexion in those days, and a man rushed up to me and asked excitedly if I was Catalan, but when I said, No, Jewish, he looked horrified and fled.

You did not say you were a Jew in the poetry world back then. The gentility of the literary world forbade it as an affront to good manners, just as proclaiming your homosexuality would be. These were things about which you kept quiet, were expected to be quietly ashamed. A number of the top poets even felt free to make anti-Semitic remarks in, and outside of, their poems, and there was no way to protest. Karl Shapiro's book *Poems of a Jew* was a shocker when it appeared.

In the late forties I wrote to T. S. Eliot asking him about the anti-Semitic passages in his poetry, and was surprised when he wrote back, saying he was "no more an anti-Semite than anti-Lapp or anti-Eskimo." But of course the evidence is there. And it was clear from his reply that he saw Jews as remote from his world of culture and refinement as the Eskimos.

≷

Every so often you have to shift gears and start writing differently. It can be a difficult period, and there are sometimes years of uncertainty until you find the new voice/subject matter/direction, and move forward again.

After my first burst of writing in Paris and Greece in 1948–49, coming back to the States froze me up. The problem: How to go on with poetry? With my life? I was in a constant state of despair, those years after returning from Europe in 1950, at being stuck in an America that, compared to the pleasures of Europe, seemed unutterably grim to me—in a period of national hysteria against everything human, the arts, political idealism. Faced with earning a living, and having no skills, I could hardly get out of bed. I had difficulty in writing at all for several years, not knowing how to go on with the direction I had started in Greece. One of the sins of my poetic generation was that every poem was supposed to be written and rewritten in the attempt to make it a masterpiece. You couldn't just write your poems, and let them be the poems of their moment, of that impulse. And I didn't know any other way.

One of my difficulties in writing was caused by a phenomenon that often occurred when I sat down to write. The words began to sing. I mean, just anything I wrote sounded like great poetry. I should have trusted it, but at that time, I couldn't believe anything that came that easily could be good. On the other hand I couldn't struggle with my poems through innumerable drafts any more. I had to change.

It was Frank O'Hara who showed me the way. Or gave me the courage to follow my instincts, accept what was happening already. In 1955, I first saw a group of his poems in *Poetry* Magazine. His sexy, surrealist poems seemed fresh and funny to me. I'd been in a new kind of psychotherapy called Group Analysis for several years and finally wised up to the fact that it

173

was against me being a poet and walked out. Luckily, I got a fellowship to Yaddo, and it was there that I discovered O'Hara's poems. When I read them to the people who gathered for drinks at the cocktail hour, they were outraged at their irresponsibility, their flaunting of homosexuality, which was just what I needed after my destructive therapy group.

After I came back to New York, I was lucky to meet Frank, far more balanced and sophisticated than I, and who took what seemed to me a casual, relaxed attitude toward his poems, writing them at lunch at the museum where he worked, as William Carlos Williams did in his office, between patients.

My poems don't really belong with what's called the New York School, but in a basic way they demonstrate an idea that I learned from Frank O'Hara at this difficult time in my life. Which was that you don't have to take a stance to write a poem—you just start from yourself, wherever you are at that moment, whatever you feel like. But the poem didn't have to be "exalted" (like a Beat poem, say), or work up to anything, unless you were in that state already. Or be a formal utterance, like the academic poetry of the time. It could just be what you were feeling at that moment, or what you might tell a friend if the telephone rang. Or if you were writing and the telephone rang, as Frank used to say, that might be the end of the poem, wherever it breaks off.

Thanks to him, I was able to get through my block, caused by my insistence that my poetry should be something other than I could do. I stopped making demands that it be anything other than what came out of me. In other words, it didn't have to be a masterpiece. Frank understood my debt to him, which I think was why he got Donald Allen to include me (though not at my best) in his anthology *The New American Poetry* among the New York Poets, with whom I hardly identify myself otherwise. Still, I'm definitely a New Yorker and a New York poet, which becomes evident to me whenever I leave New York.

It might seem obvious to say, but in writing,

> some things you let happen
> and some things you make happen.

I prefer the tender/gentle voice of Cavafy, unpretentious, natural-sounding, sensitive and yet sophisticated. Allowing the quiet feelings. I'm not interested in celebrating my highs with jazzy improvisations—maybe because I don't have that kind of highs anymore. Things just get more intense sometimes. Still,

> Writing a poem
> is giving off
> a great gust
> of energy.

Frank shared a ratty apartment on East 58th Street with another writer, Joe LeSueur. Joe (a relative of Joan Crawford, née Lucille LeSueur), had been in Gestalt Therapy with Paul Goodman, who flipped over Joe's blond Mormon good looks. Gestalt wasn't a rigid system like my Freudian group analysis had been, and there wasn't the emphasis on changing you to become a good citizen. Its goal was liberating your creative and sexual self.

> Goodman, as a Gestalt therapist,
> believed in sex with his patients.
> He used to relax them by caressing their genitals
> or fucking them.
>
> He was open about it,
> insisting sex was good for people,
> that sex didn't hurt anyone.

২৩

LIFE AMONG THE ARTISTS

In 1947 after the war, I was determined to spend the summer working on my poetry, and rented an isolated cottage on Martha's Vineyard, where I'd heard that Paul Goodman was staying in a little village across the island from me. I often bicycled by there, until one day I screwed up my nerve and knocked on his door. I knew little about Goodman at the time, except that he was an uncompromisingly avant-garde writer and social thinker who had worked with Fritz Perls to found something called Gestalt Therapy. I didn't even know that he was a poet. He, too, managed to be both married and openly gay.

It turned out that Paul Goodman was sharing a summer house with the pianist Eugene Istomin and Shirley Barab, the wife of the cellist, Seymour Barab. I joined them on the tiny beach of the hamlet, where I listened as they discussed socialism—something about original, un-soviet-style solutions to problems of a socialist economy—with Goodman, pipe clamped between his teeth, acting as the socratic teacher. While I barely recognized the names they dropped with abandon or knew anything about socialist theory, I was awed to be among intellectuals with a capital "I." That night we all went to a dance in the village hall, where Goodman ignored the fox trotting and lindy hopping of the other dancers and leaped about by himself, demonstrating the proper indifference to convention of an artistic free-spirit.

The next time I came by, a beautiful, slim young man with blond hair blowing across his brow had joined the group, and Paul Goodman was giving him his complete attention, as if he were guiding an ephebe's intellectual development and making sure that the theoretical basis of his disciple's ideas was correct. Goodman was always the teacher, with his pipe clamped between his teeth, ever the psychoanalyst-on-duty, as he discussed philosophical topics with the young, blond visitor. How I longed for the super-intellectual Paul Goodman to look at me, talk to me with more than barely-disguised tolerance. But good-looking as I was in my dark, Semitic way, Goodman was clearly dazzled by the other's WASP beauty.

I could not know that my blond "rival" would become the

176

renowned composer and diarist Ned Rorem, who would publish his diary with an account of that summer's meeting fifty years later. When I recently read the diary entry I was astonished to learn that Ned Rorem had confessed to Goodman that he was jealous of me for being so good-looking. But what makes it truly flattering was that, even before I had written anything worth reading, he thought me significant enough to record my name in his diary!

Goodman was an inveterate cruiser. He wrote that cruising was a good activity to fill in boring times, like hours of waiting at airports. Or riding in the subway. I once saw him, pipe as always between his teeth, walking through the cars of the subway train I was on, obviously killing the time on a long boring ride by checking out sexy guys.

LIVES OF THE POETS

One of Goodman's poems tells how,
after an afternoon of lovemaking
with one of his young men,
or after a stormy emotional afternoon
when someone didn't show up for a date,
or he broke up with a lover,

he would come home to dinner
and have to sit, husband and father,
at the head of the table.

Probably with that pipe clamped in his mouth!

When Brad Gooch interviewed me for his biography of Frank O'Hara, I tried to explain how different I found Frank's scene from my world. He represented a new generation. I had always seen being a writer or artist as being an outsider, a permanent freak, whereas Frank belonged to a new breed, who saw artists as part of the upper level of cultivated society, even allies of the unconventional rich. The new goal was to become a celebrity.

177

Being an artist meant building a career within the system, not on the fringe. But for us, being famous wasn't the point. Alfred Chester is a good example, someone who lived the "bohemian" life to the full and destroyed himself, destroyed the brilliant talent also. I think Brad Gooch looked at me with the uncomprehending eyes of the new generation for whom success was all. I was simply a loser to him, a leftover from the Village that was, an old man who had missed the boat.

A significant question is, Who is the poem addressed to? Other poets? (But which group of poets?) My poetry has mostly been addressed to "ordinary" people like myself (can't define this further, but am convinced on a certain level I'm ordinary, though neurotic and oddball). Not well-educated people, especially, or maybe self-educated. The current academic/establishment scene addresses its poetry to specialists, meaning other academic poets, critics, English Department élites, and the wealthy supporters of the arts. This is a world I'm pretty much out of place in. I especially can't see myself as sucking up to the rich. I don't have the least interest in being part of a social/arts scene like the Hamptons.

I'm not part of the current alliance between Capitalism and the Arts. (The way I put that sounds so old-fashioned.)

> When I'm among the rich,
> a hammer and sickle
> appears branded on my forehead,
> a red flag in my hand,
> and a chorus behind me
> sings the Internationale.
>
> On a screen in my head
> flash news reports
> of multinational headquarters
> in flames
> and the whole capitalist class
> up against the wall,
> begging for their lives.

> That's why bank vaults and pocket books
> are sealed against me,
> and munificent handouts
> go to everyone else.

But who you are writing for, who you see reading you, who you are talking to, defines your poetics—"our" kind as opposed to any other kind.

All poets are ambitious, out to make it, and there's nothing wrong with that, I tell myself, but I feel uncomfortable. It's nothing new—the Lowells/Roethkes/Berrymans were tremendous self-promoters.

Robert Lowell tried desperately to fill Eliot's shoes. Lowell also had the *orgeuil* of his name—success was to be expected in a Lowell. He was all ambition, arrogance, and determination to be a great poet. Ditto Joseph Brodsky. Whatever his poetry in Russian was, in English it was embarrassing. He had to be a creation of the Cold War.

After hearing that Susan Sontag had been denied a fellowship by a prestigious foundation, when he had written a letter of support for her application, Lowell stormed into the foundation office. "Yes, yes, Mr. Lowell," the director said, cowering before the great man. "Of course, she will get a grant." But as it turned out, Sontag had applied to a different foundation.

It's disturbing when poets are no longer outsiders. As insiders they're no longer critical of society, but part of things. In any case,

> I cannot understand a Jew
> choosing the side and the language of privilege
> instead of the underdog.

Good title for book about poetry: The Snobbery Factor. Poetry as cult product. How people give lip-service to what's in fashion, not daring to go against awesome critics like Bloom and Vendler.

> While shaving my face I answer my critics,
> marshalling rebuttals, and arguing
> my right to write as I do:
> Who are you to tell me what to do? You bastards
> don't have the least idea what poetry's about,
> etcetera…
>
> and going over and over where the chin
> makes its difficult transition to the neck:
> Why can't a clown cry real tears?
>
> Oh, I say, waving the shaver at myself,
> you pompous ass.

God knows, I don't like the poetry world. Maybe it's simply that I don't like poetry. I had read hardly any when I started writing it. And except for a few anthology pieces, what did I know of it? What drew me to it then? I still find it an effort to read. Or to sit through readings by poets. Most of it seems phony to me. Affected. Unrelated to my life.

The trouble with poets, I find, is that poetry has taken over the place of love in their hearts.

> Poets, I swear I'd throw out nine-tenths of them.
> Above all, I don't want to write like them.
> In fact, I don't want it to sound like poetry at all.

The Curse of Poetry is that it must be poetry. When I give a poetry reading, I hope they don't notice it's poetry.

> If poetry is a refuge for snobs
> any poet turning out human
> is in the nature of a miracle.

"I automatically identify with the slobs, the misfits, the victims, for whom poetry is an act of rebellion, the secret voice speaking out, however crudely." (From my statement for *The Maverick Poets*, an anthology edited by Steve Kowit)

180

Or as Gore Vidal says, "What asses they are, these poets. How fortunate that one does not have to read them."

How I envy poets of verbal complexity, or erudition, who can speak impressively about poetry and literary matters. I went to the Alliance Française to hear Donald Hall talk about his education as a poet—Exeter, Harvard, Oxford. Wrote poetry from childhood, with family encouragement. Discovered T. S. Eliot at fourteen. At sixteen began publishing in literary magazines. In his class in Harvard (Harvard again!) were Adrienne Rich, Robert Bly, Kenneth Koch, Frank O'Hara, John Ashbery (he made a point, a little too much, perhaps, of his association with O'Hara and Ashbery on the *Harvard Advocate*—they never mention him). Fifty books published. Endless awards and honors. He reads Gibbon, made a brilliant parallel between our decline in education and Rome's decline. He admires Catullus. So do I, but he really reads him, can even follow the Latin text. His imitations of Catullus are clever putdowns of people like me who cry about their lives, seek solutions in the therapies, religions, crackpot movements. And what a marvelous delivery he has, a thespian's voice that can do anything. But he made me uncomfortable, and so did the worldly, wealthy audience of professional people. It all made me feel underclass, under-educated, barely literate—and I didn't belong. I could have gone to the party afterwards. But I stole away into the night.

How different we are! Hall is the epitome of conventional success. A family man, writes about baseball, drinks with the big boys of poetry, with the English Department scholars. He visited Eliot, Pound, Frost. He has always belonged to the literary establishment, and says nothing to rock the boat.

He talked of his five years of psychoanalysis in the gap between his two marriages. He claimed it helped him immeasurably—they all claim that. After his talk I considered going up to him and congratulating him, but he was so buttoned up in his suit and tie and professional manner, and I'm just a person.

Reading his poetry, the picture of him that comes across is one of utter normality, living on the old family farm and, even though a poet, accepted by the men of his New England village as one of them, enjoying the ripeness of age, surrounded by grandchildren.

But now I learn that he's had liver cancer, and that during his recovery his wife developed leukemia and died. It must have been awful for him.

৵

From the Introduction to a new edition of *Stand Up, Friend, With Me*

Most of the poems in the first section, "Greece," I wrote on my trip to that country in 1949, while it was still in the throes of civil war. These poems had begun to emerge in a looser, conversational style even before Greek friends introduced me to the poetry of Cavafy, who also combined the colloquial tone of demotic Greek with the structure and vocabulary of the more literary tongue. Similar to his use of the vernacular, I used Yiddish intonations to soften the literary aspects in my writing. I figured that way to get in the tenderness with which Cavafy always wrote, and which Greeks used speaking to each other, as if addressing the child in each other. My poems addressed the child in the reader, and were often almost baby talk.

I had a critical experience when I went into psychotherapy —a remarkable, though unhappily brief, period of what I can only describe as a state of "expansion," and which perhaps could be clinically described as a manic phase of my manic-depressive nature, except that what I felt was almost Olympian in its openness and calm, and I would like to have remained in that state forever. The poem "A Journey" was an attempt to describe how it happened.

The title "Stand Up, Friend, With Me" was from a poem (not included in the book) that I wrote during this period, which began, mysteriously, when my father offered me money (symbolic of love?). It was very much like the plot of Dostoievsky's novel, *A Raw Youth*, in which an illegitimate son experiences a tremendous liberation after he is recognized by his natural father. I, too, felt

182

recognized by my father, and something opened up in me that had been closed and I *stood up*. The words have a magical, though exact, meaning for me. Perhaps I was crazy, but I felt sane for the first time in my life. It was not a state of bliss, or a high, just wonderful to be able to breathe so easily, feel part of other men, feel perfectly okay for the first time in my life.

Various critics have interpreted the title, *Stand Up, Friend, with Me*, in different ways, as referring to my teacher, Robert Friend, or, more amusingly, the "friend" as the Freudian "little friend," a synonym for my penis. Actually, the "friend" of the title refers to every underdog in the world, inviting them to join me in my new pride in myself, my newfound courage to *stand up* against whatever or whoever is oppressing them. But this wonderful state did not last. It was real, but it soon went away, never to return.

Difficult as it was to sit down and write, in the gloomy years that followed, I did manage to write a poem a day for some time at the office I worked in, usually starting with the spectacular view out the window of the Hudson River and the New Jersey shore. I tried to imagine the world across the river as "other" than the world I was in, this world I couldn't deal with. But I couldn't make it the Europe where I had been so happy and discovered how to write just a few years before. All I dreamed of was to return, but couldn't get the money.

Most of the poems in *Stand up, Friend, with Me* chart psychological victories, insights, snatched from the muddle of the depression that I suffered from for years. They usually represent moments of the opening up of feelings, the opposite of the deadness of depression, and end with a fragment of hope, dearly won, even if transitory. But perhaps the poems in the fourth section of the book, A New Cycle, have a slightly greater margin of optimism.

The last poem, "The Garden," is a celebration of finding a companion in life and how it changed everything. Even so, it was a long time before my suffering became tolerable. It helped that I had to think of someone else for a change, and put myself aside to a great extent. Before this, I had only thought of myself as a

183

public person, never a private one. But when I moved in with my friend, it meant that I didn't have to live a life of hell any more—symbolically, as a scapegoat or the voice of mankind, or play the prophet role, which I was not really suited for anyway.

The poems in this first book were written between 1949 and 1962, and perhaps it is just as well that I didn't succeed in getting a publisher earlier, since, with new poems being added all the time, the manuscript kept getting stronger. But years of rejection took their toll, and when I won the Lamont Award in 1962, I kept repeating, "I will not be consoled." But I was. My life changed considerably. For one thing, I could make a living—I gave poetry readings around the country, wrote narrations for a couple of documentary films, translated a book of Eskimo poems, and, yes, even taught poetry workshops for a while.

Stand Up, Friend, With Me: Though I no longer expect it to be emblazoned on the banner of the revolution, I heard that it was on a placard carried in a Gay Pride march, several years ago. Some people get the message.

ॐ

SECRETS OF THE CLOSET

At Amherst, James Merrill was having an affair with his poetry teacher, Kimon Friar, who at that time was also running the Poetry Center at the 92nd Street YMHA in New York. When Merrill's gorgon of a mother got wind of it, she called Kimon Friar to her townhouse on Sutton Place and had a showdown with him. It was soon after that that Kimon left Amherst and the Poetry Center and sailed for Greece for good, with a windfall from Jimmy's wealthy mother.

After Jimmy graduated from college, his father, of the Wall Street brokerage house of Merrill, Lynch, Fenner, and Beane, asked him what he wanted to do next. When Jimmy said to be a poet, the senior Mr. Merrill took him up the elevator in the skyscraper of his Wall Street headquarters and presented him, as a graduation present, with an office with his name on the door,

184

where he could practice his new profession in a style befitting the son of a tycoon.

In later years, Merrill's boyish face developed the indomitable jaw of a dowager and became strangely withered like an unwrapped mummy. When *The Changing Light of Sandover* was being filmed, a friend wrote me, Merrill resorted to "the magical Flash Effet Beauté. A colorless liquid, it comes in an ampoule to be broken open and applied rapidly to the whole face. Presto! Change-o! It did wonders for him on camera."

I think with rare exceptions, like Warhol, successful people in the arts come from money, go to Harvard, have cultivated backgrounds.

In the early fifties when I first met John Ashbery through Frank O'Hara, they were best friends and thought and even wrote very much alike, but Frank was obviously becoming the power center of their world in New York. In his autobiography, *What Did I Do?*, Larry Rivers says, "Frank and John were always neck and neck in the writing steeplechase, and until then there was no declared winner. It kept things hot and funny between them for years." I suspect that John worked out with his analyst the solution of going to Paris and salvaging his ego by making his career there, leaving New York to Frank. It was after Frank's death that Ashbery returned to this country, the throne vacant, and with Vendler and Bloom behind him, his poetry swept the field.

I remember a review in which Vendler even said with satisfaction that Ashbery writes as well as Wallace Stevens, but had dispensed with the content. She must have the same feeling about Stevens' philosophical musings as I do. In spite of the charm of his poetry, I dislike him as a person and it poisons his poems for me.

A good analysis of Ashbery (from "Uneven Pavement" by Evelyn McDonnell, *San Francisco Chronicle*, 19 April 1997): "The band members are to modern rock what John Ashbery is to American poetry: clever, well-read influence-distillers who deftly create

185

moments that sound like epiphanies but leave the listener unchanged."

Our most famous poets, like Merrill and Ashbery, write as though the world they're part of is one in which concentration camps don't/couldn't exist.

Yet, Lou Asekoff told me that at a Vietnam War read-in at Riverside Church in the early 70s he saw John Ashbery cry while reading from Walt Whitman's notes on nursing wounded soldiers. Is that evidence of a living heart?

I'm always trying to figure out Ashbery's strange mentality. Sometimes I think he views writing poetry as a flight from a hotly pursuing reader, so that he must keep dodging, doubling back, switching over, every time you start to follow him. Then, as he says, he likes to sneak out just before the poem is over. Yet with all the complex maneuvering, it is always, remarkably, the same voice, the same person we are conscious of tracking. We recognize his tracks, his tricks, his jokes, for he clearly has fun playing this game, in spite of what some voice inside must be telling him, that poetry is not a game, at least not a game like that, and that the heart yearns to reveal itself, or at least the child in us wants to cry out directly. Of course, he'd titter at this, being far more sophisticated than me. And maybe it's not true for him.

He's built an aesthetics on offhand remarks.

Ashbery and O'Hara and Kenneth Koch started a school of New York chatter, and like chatter, it is often inconsequential. But fun.

I feel like saying to him: John, stop changing the subject.

He keeps exhibiting his superiority over the rest of us, though mercifully, his saving grace is his trashy edge. His is certainly not a poetry of seeking mutual ground with others. You have to

186

admire the virtuosity, but in him it becomes almost a monstrous quality.

But that is what Modern Poetry was always about, sneering at the common herd, fleeing the banalities of Kansas and Idaho, the "philistines." (Mystery: Young poets are not anti-American anymore!) The great ones—Eliot, Stevens, even Frost—proclaim in their poetry their glittering icy uniqueness, and the world has enshrined them. With Eliot, mandarin poetry took over and, through the Eastern establishment, continues to dominate to this day. Ashbery is very much in that tradition.

Of course, poetry really has an inner elite. There is no democracy of standards in poetry, nor should be.

To be a successful poet today you have to be very sophisticated, smooth, unassailable, impervious to ridicule, superior, defended, self-referential.

One amazing thing about John Ashbery's career and ascension to the throne, vacant since Eliot, is that unlike Eliot who wrote endless critical works, laying down his theories of aesthetics and culture to intimidate us slobs, Ashbery, except for his old art criticism, writes no prose, no reviews, nothing but poetry.

The quality that unites the poets of Frank O'Hara's world is in allowing fun into poetry. But with Kenneth Koch it goes sour. He has a Little Mary Sunshine complex. It is a manic humor, but the nastiness creeps out around the edges. One of his Columbia students said he wanted to do a report on my poetry, and Koch said, "Not in my class."

I try to go to the poetry reading that the Academy of American Poets holds every year for their big donors at the Morgan Library, featuring a celebrity poet, a really impressive event in such opulent surroundings. Last year, the featured poet was

187

Seamus Heaney. He's all right, but he's cautious, like straight men often are.

This year (1997) it was John Ashbery. He was introduced by Richard Howard, who was brilliant—compared Ashbery, or rather the trajectory of his career, to Wordsworth and Stevens—like them, dismissed and ridiculed by critics at first and ending up on coffee tables and in backpacks. When Ashbery came on, he said that was a hard act to follow, and it was true. His reading was terrible—started poems with "This is...," and read too fast, without expression. But he was charming when he explained where he got his whimsical titles. About the poems, all I can say is, Ashbery was ... Ashbery. They could be dismissed as doodling, a game of trivia, except for the genuine voice of the poet. But is that enough? It's obvious he takes writing seriously, since he's been doing the same thing for 50 years, but he doesn't want you to think he's taking it seriously.

Mostly, this was an opportunity to see him, and it was clearly an historic occasion. The audience gave him an ovation before and after, applauding him for his celebrity—another instance of being famous for being famous. He really enjoyed the tribute, and I didn't begrudge him.

At a poetry reading, why are Intros so often more interesting than the poems they introduce? Our task should be to put that material into the poems.

Rules for readings:
    Don't introduce poems with "This is."
    Don't leaf through papers trying to decide what to read
        next.
    Don't arrive late.
    Don't read too fast. Read slowly. Poetry's hard to get.
    Don't smile at your in-jokes. (Ashbery's crowd does this.)
    Make sure the mike is working.

꙳

SECRETS OF THE CLOSET

In the sixties I was at a literary conference that included a well-known poet, a modern man of letters—and undeniably straight. My first two books had some openly gay poems and I was known to be gay—this was before Gay Liberation had been officially declared, but there was a new freedom in the air. The day I arrived, the bearded man of letters had just finished his part in the conference, and we only met briefly in the evening at a social gathering.

Late that night in the campus guest house, I'd just gotten into bed when there was a knock on my door and the portly, bearded poet was standing there, obviously drunk—poets were expected to get drunk in those days. I asked what he wanted. "I'd like to sleep with you," he answered. This came out of the blue, and, stupefied, I asked, "Why?" "To make love to you." I declined politely, though as soon as I'd shut the door, I regretted that I hadn't invited him in. He was probably going through a rocky period and was ready to experiment. I should have tried to help him by getting him to open up and talk about it, but I was too tired after my trip and needed to be up early for a morning session.

≈

Introduction to new edition of Tu Fu

When I discovered the poetry of Tu Fu, I knew instantly I had found a master. I was already obsessed with the poetry of Constantine Cavafy, who even in translation, has a recognizable voice. Like Cavafy, Tu Fu used deceptively plain language and few devices, and it seemed to me that, in English, Tu Fu also sounded very much like himself, though he lived over a thousand years ago. Poet as human being—rare in poetry.

It was in the early sixties that I bought my first collection of Tu Fu, published by the Foreign Languages Press in Beijing, at the Chinese government bookshop on lower Fifth Avenue in New York City. The translator, Rewi Alley, I was told by the poet Millen Brand, was a New Zealander living in Beijing. This seemed an unusual, even daring, place to go at that time of the cold war. During the fifties, a number of Americans, leftists and homosexuals, had escaped persecution to more hospitable countries, if they were lucky enough to skip out before their passports were lifted. A few, courageous, perhaps, or perhaps foolhardy, refused like Millen Brand to cooperate with the government interrogators and became outcasts and hence unemployable. But many major artists turned state's evidence, swept up in the hysteria that the United States was being taken over by subversives, or perhaps just protecting their asses. Following a phone call from Robert Lowell, in one of his crazy phases, that Yaddo was a nest of communists, the F.B.I. swept down in a raid on the arts colony, and terrorized everyone.

More than the execution of the Rosenbergs, that assault on Yaddo symbolized the decade for me, when artists were taught such a bitter lesson for meddling in politics—painters retreated to the safety of abstract expressionism, poets were told the only fit subjects were carousels and angels, and analysts tried to turn their queer patients straight. It was against this background that I breathed in Tu Fu's free spirit. He wrote not only about politics, but was not afraid of being sentimental. He felt it was within his competence, indeed his duty as a poet, to advise rulers on how to deal with his country's problems, a country in turmoil, although they listened as little in 8th century China as they listen to poets here.

The poetry of Tu Fu seemed to me a major departure from the fuzzily mystic poems in the Arthur Waley anthology that gave my generation its idea of "oriental" poetry. Or the fragments of Chinese classics in the bombastic Cantos by the detestable Ezra Pound. Tu Fu's poetry doesn't need to be read any special way to make it poetry. In that, it is modern: You just say it. He is down to earth like Chekhov in his feeling for human suffering and his observations of life. But like Cavafy, he is among the most elegant poets of history. Quite appropriate to this view of him, though perhaps not to the puritanical Chinese government, is Carolyn Kizer's clever sequence of quatrains, a letter from Tu Fu to his friend and fellow poet, Li Po, that begins:

190

Milord, how beautifully you write!
May I sleep with you tonight?
Till I flag, or when thou wilt,
we'll roll up, drunken, in one quilt....

Kizer is but one of the many poets who have written about and/or translated Tu Fu. But while making Tu Fu very human, this poem does seem to perpetuate the contemporary cliché of Chinese sages as drunks, perhaps to justify our own tradition of the poet as self-destructive lush. In oriental traditions, however, drunkenness is a code word for the ecstasy of spirit, which comes about not necessarily from alcohol and drugs. I once heard a story about May Swenson being driven to the outskirts of Tucson to watch the dawn come up over the Arizona hills dotted with giant saguaro cactuses with their upraised arms, like lonely sentinels of the Cargo Cult of New Guinea waiting for the return of World War II supply planes to spill out treasures again. As the sun's rays burst over the landscape, Richard Shelton told me that May was so carried away that she fell to the ground and rolled around, much as a worshipper at a dervish ceremony I attended in Kabul fell into a seizure-like trance at the climax of the chanting.

Of course, it is possible to select among the hundreds of surviving poems and construct the Tu Fu you want. Some selections make him the inebriate, others an Arthur Waley mystic, but this choice of poems seems a balanced one, both public and private, showing him as a man at the center of a turbulent era, more out of favor with emperors than in, and mostly banished to the countryside, a destiny which had the virtue, as Lenin once said about being in prison, of giving him the chance to write. But even far from the center of power he is always trying to solve social problems, worrying about the homeless, the sick, and the hungry. Read in this context, the poems communing with nature are welcome as relief from the crowded landscape, full of armies and refugees, full of human suffering.

Tu Fu's influence is so powerful that I believe anyone who reads him can write a wonderful poem of his own immediately afterwards. For a brief moment, bathed in the light of his spirit, we have the feeling that poetry is indeed alive within us, and our thoughts flow on a wave of feeling directly to the page. But only one such poem is given. For there are no short cuts in this difficult art, and we again face, this time by ourselves, all the problems of writing poetry, once the illusion of simplicity that Tu Fu creates in us, much like the first, dizzy belief in communism as the obvious answer to all the world's problems, vanishes.

*

Before this generation, E. E. Cummings was the only American poet who could get away with humor in his poetry (though it was satirical humor) and still not be classed with Ogden Nash as Light Verse. Even more sensational, he used the word fucking, which was printed in anthologies as "I will not kiss your f.ing flag."

Besides Cummings, I could of course look to W. H. Auden with sassy or funny lines, jingles, and openly queer references, as in "He's marvelous/he's Greek./When I see him/my knees go weak." This was liberating in the otherwise stuffy age of the New Criticism.

I was immediately attracted to poets who sounded like recognizable human beings, and in this category I do not include Marianne Moore, T. S. Eliot, John Crowe Ransom, Allen Tate, et al., whatever their literary virtues. Pound sometimes sounded human, if obnoxiously so, when he wasn't putting on a fake archaic tone or railing like a country preacher. Hart Crane was a legend for being openly gay among a bunch of stuffed shirts, though in his poetry only in the moments of self pity did he come through. Wallace Stevens belonged with "spiritual" people, conservatives, and anti-Semites. And Frost had a folksy voice I didn't cotton to until later when I stopped worshipping everything self-consciously literary and modern.

*

LIVES OF THE POETS

When he was a teenager
Robert Duncan ran away
to New York City.
Homeless and broke,
he hung around a bar near Penn station
where commuters stopped in after work.

One of them would take him
to a hotel for a quickie
before going home to the suburbs,
and he'd have a room for the night.

૨ఆ

LIVES OF THE POETS

Amy Clampitt, Mona Van Duyn, and Marguerite Young decided that after graduation from their midwest university they would go live in New York. (Marguerite Young told me this story on Bleecker Street one day—I always used to run into her on the streets of the Village wearing her flapping long skirts and shawl.) The other two did get there, but Van Duyn, changing trains in Chicago, couldn't make herself go any further, and ended up spending her life in St. Louis.

While Marguerite was still a student in the mid-west, she told me she shared an apartment with Jean Garrigue. But seeing from my look that I assumed they had been lovers, she quickly started telling me how she seduced one of her professors.

૨ఆ

Review of *Nature: Poems Old and New*, by May Swenson
(Published in *Exquisite Corpse*)

Many admirable poets, poets I like, are forgotten after their deaths—I'm thinking of Millen Brand and Dunstan Thompson, for instance. But thanks to the efforts of her literary executor,

Zan Knudson, May Swenson's books continue to appear.

It wasn't that she was ignored in her lifetime. She had little trouble finding publishers, received numerous honors, and even a shower of gold at the end in the form of a MacArthur fellowship. She once told me that it made her nervous when poets got money. But she came from a time when there was no money in it, when poets were hardly more than a cliquish handful, intense and exclusive. Money was not to be mentioned in connection with poetry. Her generation of poets was obsessed with being pure. Forget writing for the movies! Even writing a novel was considered selling out, though some things didn't lessen your prestige, like writing reviews, or academic work, or working for one of the major publishers. It was considered shocking, though, when poets like John Ciardi and James Dickey got rich, but by then, things were already going downhill for the poetry world with its so-called "standards." The gates were open and the raw multitudes were pouring through.

When I met her, May was a reader of manuscripts at New Directions Press, which published the New Directions annuals—I'd been in several issues. She got the publisher James Laughlin to submit my manuscript for the Lamont Award, which, anyway, I didn't win that year. The inflexible rule of that era was that you could only submit your manuscript to one publisher at a time, and often they kept it for months, if not years. It seems odd to me now that I only submitted to the major publishers who kept rejecting me. But small presses didn't exist for me then. I wanted to be published by the publishers of the great. By the time I was in my mid-thirties I had already gotten a couple of dozen rejections on my manuscript, when May advised me to forget the rules and make multiple submissions. I did, sent the book to half a dozen publishers at once, and it worked. Within a year I had a contract, and along with the book, a major award (the Lamont) and a Guggenheim fellowship.

The latest collection of May Swenson, a representative selection of poems under the rubric of Nature, is a good introduction. Don't get misled by the naked hetero couple on the book jacket—though come to think of it, sex is sex and that's a luscious full-frontal view of a lady dying to surrender, which is appropriate for May Swenson's sensual poetry. And skip the Foreword, like a deadly sprinkle of roach killer, though the examples quoted are well-chosen. One of the qualities of May Swenson's poetry is that it is easy to quote—you can open the book anywhere and find lines that are fun. Sometimes it's too cutesie-pie, like Emily Dickinson, but on the whole May had powerful things to say.

> Stop bleeding said the knife.
> I would if I could   said the cut.

Minds accustomed to the flat directness and straight narration of Charles Bukowski might have to concentrate harder to get her, wrestle with her elaborate language, for this is a different order of poetry. But don't be put off. She's writing "poetry," which is generally thought to demand a certain amount of metaphor, fancy description. That, admittedly, is hard for any poet to resist. As well as that other temptation of poetry, word play. But outside of slowing you up with conundrum-like statements, these poems are not difficult. They're fun to figure out.

A true modern, May's mind is often on sex in all its aspects, like how nature is all sex. And there is actually quite a lot of entertaining dykery going on under the guise of bees sipping flowers, that sort of thing, much like our premier lesbian poet, Emily Dickinson. And as in Dickinson, the pronouns are often the convenient he-she, though it doesn't mask anything: "A bee rolls in the yellow rose./Does she invite his hairy rub?"

I used to go to parties at May Swenson's apartment on Perry Street in the Village, where she lived with her first partner, Pearl, though there may have been a couple of others before I met her. Surely not more than a couple, because May was serially monogamous, and lived a stable, even sedate existence, with no crazy love affairs, Brazilian escapades, mental hospital stays, or wild drinking bouts at the White Horse to create a legend. As a fallen-away Mormon she was always plagued by the Mormon kids on their missionary year ringing her doorbell, so she had to take her name off the door, but she wasn't an ex-Mormon-gone-wild, like a fellow airman of mine in the Eighth Air Force, who came back from passes in London with eyes crossed from guilt over his sexual adventures. Whenever Mormon missionaries come to my door with their shining faces, I remember that blond, handsome pilot, and am tempted to invite them in and make their missionary year a true learning experience.

Through the years at May's parties at the Perry Street apartment, I met lots of literary figures, like John Hall Wheelock, Babette Deutsch, Jean Garrigue, and Howard Moss. At her gay parties I met her other world, which she didn't hide and of course overlapped with her literary side, as is evident in the poems. At the memorial service after her death, the auditorium was filled with a mind-boggling mixture of Mormons, literary people, dykes and queers.

Outside of a few poets like Auden and Hart Crane, I don't think I could have stood the founders of modern poetry. But I'm even more uncomfortable with the poets of May's generation, like Robert Lowell and Elizabeth Bishop and John Berryman and Theodore Roethke, all of them, except for May, politicking for position and rewards, which they got, though always acting like it just came to them out of the blue. What a bunch of hypocrites! They were all jockeying to become King of Poetry after T. S. Eliot's death. But May stayed clear of all that. She remained honest, which might be why she is less prominent today than the others are, when she is clearly the better poet. In fact, she is practically the only one whose poetry I still can read from that generation. Critics crow nowadays, along with the victory of corporate capitalism, about poetry being about language. "Language is and has always been my principal interest, my principal concern, my principal delight," wrote Jean Stafford. I feel that's mostly a bullshit fiat laid down to keep poetry tame.

Still, if May Swenson's poetry fulfills that rule, thank God she goes beyond it. Her poetry is a human utterance I respond to, and is why I remain heavily in debt to it. She can teach anyone lessons in being specific, exact, and sticking to the facts. But then she jumps overboard in wild cosmic speculation. The shaped poems are truly clever, one of the rare instances since

196

Cummings in which typography adds to the effect of poetry. I once went to a reading at the YMHA where May had the poems projected on a screen as she read them, which proved it was not just a gimmick, but added a dimension.

May Swenson once told me I was a true poet. It's my turn to say that she was a true poet, and these poems collected by her true friend Zan Knudson demonstrate it.

From my tribute at May Swenson memorial at the NY Historical Society

"Though she left the Village many years before her death, May will always be a Villager for me—I mean part of the old Village that has disappeared. She lived for years on Perry Street, one of the quintessential Village streets where most Villagers lived, as opposed to the more obvious tourist scene of Christopher, MacDougal, or Eighth Street. After working at her desk all morning, she liked to go out for lunch to Bigelow's Drug Store, a short walk away on Sixth Avenue and Ninth Street, where she would meet literary friends like Jean Garrigue and Ursule Molinaro at the lunch counter.

"Oddly, May's moving away coincided with the end of the Village as The Village, for it was about that time that it became a high rent neighborhood that young artists couldn't afford, and the arts activities moved to the so-called East Village. I still live there, but I've only been able to stay thanks to the subsidized artists' housing project, Westbeth. May once stayed for a time in my studio there, and wrote "Staying at Ed's Place," that was published in the *New Yorker*.

"May wanted to move back to the Village, and was even looking for a co-op, but I'm sure she would have been disappointed, for hardly anyone she knew is left, and in its essence the Village has changed. Even the lunch counter at Bigelow's is gone, as well as the Riker's on Eighth Street that she wrote about in 'Snow In New York,' a poem that recaptures for me the old Village days...."

As I read the poem I felt the whole auditorium literally fall in love with me. I got high on it. The audience was half May's

Mormon clan from Utah and the other half her lesbian crowd, all of them at their most ladylike. But her friends were never the biker types anyway. Her two longtime partners were there, Zan on one side of the room and Pearl on the other.

Most of the poems read by the other speakers in the program I would have chosen myself. They had a new power, which must have something to do with them being on their own, now that their creator is dead.

෬

NOTES AFTER DAVID BERGMAN INTERVIEW
(in *American Poetry Review*)
The word processor has made it possible to write down a lot of the ideas I get, which I never could face doing before, because they come out in scattershot confusion, and on the screen it is so much easier to straighten out the mess than with a typewriter. The screen is useful for prose, especially. I've already done pieces on Berlin, visiting Paul Bowles (published in *Raritan*), renting flats in different cities abroad (which we often do), several essays about Alfred Chester (*NY Times Book Review/Boston Review*), an essay about Southern California poetry called "Neo Pop, the New Populist Poetry" (*Poets and Writers*), a play about AIDS, etc.

Alfred Chester has been another of my obsessions—to get him back in print. I feel as though I'm rescuing part of my life.

My generation had the idea, an imperative, that you must destroy yourself for your art (like Hart Crane). It meant working for posterity, not the present. I barely survived, though my friend Alfred Chester destroyed himself, true to the dictum.

The problem of survival as a poet (until I got published) I made more painful and difficult, since according to the romantic notions of the time, getting a steady job would have meant selling out. Actually, once I started to work and support myself, I was even able to write on the job, as so many others discovered before

198

me—Frank O'Hara, W. C. Williams, Stevens, and all those university teacher poets.

I don't feel comfortable with the idea of poetry as part of university life, a subject in the curriculum. Lots of poets, the majority, find shelter in that world, but it is an alien atmosphere for me. I don't combine scholarship with poetry, and don't feel as a poet that I must. Of course, I was a terrible student, and a dropout.

In 1949 when I dropped out of NYU and went to Paris, it was the cheapest place to go, and my God, what you got for your money! So I was quite surprised by the Beat explosion in San Francisco. I knew guys who went there for sex, but I was only interested in Paris, culture capitol of the world. The Beats were doing something like I did—poetry for the voice, using forbidden language and subject matter. For the first time you could be Jewish, and openly gay. I didn't share their anarchist style, however, with its noisy effects.

In '49, I had had this tremendous experience in Greece, feeling an identity with the people, discovering Cavafy, and learning the Greek language. It was a country where for the first time I felt comfortable with myself.

Whenever I'm in a place where a different language is spoken, I feel a wonderful sense of possibility. English seems in its vocabulary and syntax stacked against me.

I haven't been a good manager of my literary life: The New Poems section, "The Crier" (in *New and Selected Poems*, published by Sheep Meadow Press), was originally a manuscript, much longer, that I wanted to be called EXODOS, which means "The Way Out" in Greek. Then, when the manuscript evolved into the *New and Selected* it was supposed to be called *From the Book of My Life*, but there was a screw up, and it was listed with the Library of Congress as just *New and Selected Poems*, so that's the title on the book jacket.

The Buddhist/Christian Science principle that "there is no error in the universe" is greatly comforting to a hypochondriac like me. I have a long series of poems about hypochondria and others about the horrors of aging, but such subjects turn editors, and maybe everybody, off. You are supposed to find spiritual wisdom in age, not complain. Poets are expected to sound like poetry has brought them illumination—or just write about those moments. The implication is that we are spiritual masters.

Why I'm not a "gay" poet: In my generation, Sexual Freedom was seen as the key issue, with the idea that Gay Liberation was included. (See my poem "Graffiti.") As it turned out, when sexual liberation didn't include gays, the gay movement became a political necessity.

Am I a gay poet? I'm gay, a Jew, and a lefty—in other words, I feel oppressed on several counts.

Instead of a life dedicated to help mankind, it turned out that I chose a life of service to one person. When I moved back in with my friend after he lost his sight, it was the first time in my life I felt really useful, and it changed my life. Gradually, this responsibility (not wanting to leave him alone for long) and dislike of the visiting-poet routine at colleges ended my poetry reading tours. It also led to working with him on fiction and screenplays, which is fun. And I was amazed how much money we made on our novel *Village* (published under our pseudonym, Bruce Elliot). But it happened only that one time.

Fiction has long boring stretches, tedium. Poetry leaves that out.

I, and many poets now, violate the boundary between high and low culture. David Trinidad says that Frank O'Hara and I were first to start using what he calls pop material. I imagine he means my movie poems.

It always surprised me when people laughed at my poems, when all I was doing was telling the grim truth. Laughter is really a form of recognition of truth.

I have to say again that my poems often embarrass me.

≥●

Everybody seems to say that poetry should be this, or it should be that. The thing is that almost all poets will promote their own kind of poetry. But I resent anyone trying to legislate what poetry is, or what it's for. I trust what teenagers see in poetry, why they are attracted to it. It has something to do with poetry as magic. It also has to do with an idealism that gets lost as you get older, especially if you get involved in the poetry world with its ugly political conflicts. When I started writing, I first wanted poetry to save the world, I would stand up in the marketplace and my words would inspire the multitudes. And then when I lost that faith, I desperately wanted poetry to save me, which it actually did. I still believe poetry is a kind of magic.

Why does the eye slide over the poetry in magazines? It must be because you have to slow down to read it, and that's hard to do. It feels like hard work. But once you learn to slow down, if you can bear to slow down, you begin to see what you've been missing reading prose, racing through sentences for "meaning." You find out what's special about poetry.

It's like the difference between calisthenics and yoga: It's mostly slowing down. The movements are practically the same, and both are strenuous. Doing yoga, though, you can pay more attention to what's going on. It's just that some people are calisthenics people who need vigorous movement and some are yoga people, just as some people are prose people and some are poetry people.

≥●

NOTES: GOING TO SCHOOL AT THE MOVIES
(published in *Telescope*)

As much as poetry has fought against gentility, against being tagged a ladies club art practiced by ladies with three names, which was at least part of the reason for the modernist revolution early in the century, gentility keeps creeping back in. The academic world also keeps appropriating poetry with its own kind of respectability, and poetry again becomes "high culture" separating it from "low," and by extension, "low class." If rescued from the sentimental, the poetry becomes grown up, about grown up things. I always felt people became poets and highbrows especially to obliterate the dumb kids they were, bury the misery of the past, hiding the unacceptable self, the anguish of being a jerk, behind the mask of the poet, the intellectual. How I still admire anyone able to succeed at doing that, transforming oneself, though I'm incapable of it myself.

Of course, a high, refined style is rarely popular and why should it be? The pioneers of modern poetry were not populists. They understood the power of an elite, even if they started as iconoclasts.

When I started writing, poetry was strictly opposed to "debased" pop culture—except for occasional cult figures like Charlie Chaplin and Krazy Kat. Movies (perhaps exempting French movies) were lowbrow—as indeed they are, but were dismissed for that reason, in spite of being enjoyed. What hypocrites we were back then! Highbrow was opposed to everything lowbrow—in public. (Leading to odd judgments that because you enjoy something, or weep over it, doesn't mean it's good!) Language especially had to be distorted any way necessary to appear unusual, and if anything popular was mentioned it was with irony.

With the new populist spirit in the arts in the 60s, an influence from the movies on poetry grew visible. In painting, artists from working-class backgrounds like Andy Warhol reproduced the symbols of pop culture we all grew up with. Alfred Chester, in a letter in 1964, wrote that Pop Art was "the triumph of the things that had meaning for us in our childhood ... all the things we loved

202

as children.... Art needs a dip into vulgarity to give it life."

I myself, like others, rebelled against my generation's poetry of the cultivated man, and insisted on writing out of what I couldn't deny, that at bottom I was still little Eddie Field of Lynbrook, starstruck, fucked up, and with a language that came out of my immigrant Jewish background. (I didn't know back then that Jewish was special.) And what was his poetry? Movie plots, dirty and romantic fantasies, impossibly old-fashioned sentimental poems about poor, helpless creatures, and endless psychological problems with family, sex, Jewishness—none of which editors wanted poetry to be about. It was too bad that I wasn't the intellectual I'd hoped to be, but I came to accept that I was stuck with what I was.

When I started writing, poets commonly used Greek myths, often in a modern interpretation—Auden's "Icarus," to give a splendid example—or dragged biblical or classical allusions into the poem to give it an air of profundity, or for a resounding finish. An extreme example is Richard Eberhart's famous groundhog poem that ends with references to China, Greece, Alexander, Montaigne, and Saint Theresa!

It came to me, then, that there was no reason not to use movies as a source of mythology, a frame of reference.

But why retell a story already seen and more vivid on the screen? Because personal associations and how you remember it, not as it was, make the meaning of the story different, make the story your own. I had seen most of the movies I wrote about years before, so what stuck with me was already shaped by the idiosyncrasy of memory. Just as mythology grows in the retelling through generations. I think I'm justified in assuming that others have seen the same movies I have, or similar ones, and can appreciate my poem-versions.

Besides, these stories didn't start with the movies. "Frankenstein" goes back in history via Mary Shelley to the Hebrew Golem, alchemist legends like Faust, and further. (Though in my poems I'm not interested in explaining all that—it's implicit.) The meaning of Frankenstein, for example, keeps changing. Relevant to us for its depiction of the underdog, its symbolism of racism and our sexual split, it once was a fantasy of revenge for an oppressed people.

ᔫ

The Problem of Form: The discovery in my movie poems that narrative could hold a poem together—the rediscovery of narrative as structure for poetry.

Answer to "Questions of Accent" by Murat Nemet-Nejat
(Exquisite Corpse)

I eagerly followed the brilliant argument of Murat Nemet-Nejat on the discontinuity of tradition in American poetry. Like him, I see our myths in the offerings of pop culture, and identify with their style and tone and language. For lack of a decent education, pop culture is all we have, though it is richer than pop artists present it.

Where I part company with Mr. Nemet-Nejat is when he attacks poetry as merely a reflection of or homage to pop culture, if I follow him correctly. But can't we reclaim the culture and transform it into the genuine? As an old-fashioned lefty, I see the purpose of poetry right now as opposing the plastic myth and offering a genuine alternative. Even if it's already too late.

There is so much meretricious language, thinking, and feeling around. Yet there is a folk expression which is genuine, colorful. If one way of poetry is to be superior, elitist, the other is to rescue the clichés, the banal, whatever is vigorous in the popular language and culture.

ᔫ

ON SOUTHERN CALIFORNIA POETRY

From Richard Howard's introduction to *Maps to Anywhere* by Bernard Cooper

"Movies and radio, television and malls—these constitute the culture which affords the imagery Cooper deploys; no

204

theater, no art, no music to sweeten the spirit's functions. And being Jewish—in Los Angeles, at least—is no help at all; where, one may ask, are the people of the Book? No, the camera and the internal-combustion engine are the alpha and omega of this world."

"Certainly this is prose...not derived from vestiges of culture..., here is a self-begotten American dialect...."

From a Lecture for *Writers on Writing* series, Mid-Manhattan Library

During a radio interview recently, I found myself stumped by one question. I was asked why my poetry was especially popular in Long Beach. I have plenty of fans around the country, but Gerald Locklin says he considers me one of the "fathers" of Long Beach poetry, along with Charles Bukowski. The interviewer said she thought that this was somewhat strange since I'm very much a New York poet, and the west coast doesn't usually think much of New York's literary tastes. Bukowski and I even have the same publisher. I could only come up with an inept explanation, and ever since, I've been trying to work out what I might have said.

With Bukowski's death, I've been thinking about the unsuccessful interview even more. Bukowski is a curious figure in the poetry world. While he's pretty much ignored in the Northeast as a poet, he was the (unofficial) poet laureate of southern California and widely read in the rest of the country. His books are best-sellers in Germany, and all over Europe he's considered one of the best American poets. Some of the obituaries that a friend sent from England are far more laudatory than the grudging, almost embarrassed acknowledgment of his achievements in the New York Times.

He was the old-fashioned kind of bohemian artist who thumbed his nose at society from a position on the bottom, which is very much out of fashion now. But he became a success in spite of himself. Or was he always aiming for success, as one feels the Beats were? With all their railing at society weren't they playing the fame game? But what's wrong with it, especially if you don't compromise? Why do I keep feeling that the only moral position for a poet is outside? The pride, the honor, in being on the bottom has disappeared. Or perhaps being on top is also okay, it's being in the nowhere middle that should be scorned.

Surveying the poetry scene it almost seems that Bukowski stood alone as the counterweight to the academic/formalist tradition that is dominant today. Even more than the Beats, the other wing of anti-establishment poetry, Bukowski represents the bohemian, radical, non-academic tradition. Radical for him, though, meant a sour rejection of any political belief. He stubbornly refused to be part of bourgeois society, or play along with the literary game. And he hasn't been adopted by academe. He continues to be very hard for them to swallow.

He makes poetry accessible to anybody. That is a very radical notion.

Compared to Bukowski, I'm a starry-eyed idealist, a softy. I've been published in the respectable magazines that would never publish him, or even review him. I belong to both ends of the spectrum.

For people like us, poetry doesn't belong to academia. We were before the era of poetry workshops and MFA programs. The granddaddies of poetry workshops existed at Iowa and Stanford, but I wouldn't have had anything to do with them, even if I could get in. The masters of modern poetry who are taught in poetry classes today never studied in workshops either, but learned to write by themselves. Writers of "creative writing" as it was called then, writers in all fields, learned to write on their own. Novelists, playwrights, essayists—Truman Capote, Tennessee Williams, Gore Vidal, James Baldwin—also learned by themselves. Today, MFA programs turn out skilled technicians by the thousands, but in the flood of books resulting, there's nothing much worth reading.

Nowadays bohemianism is generally devalued and "Greenwich Village poet," as I've been called in the *NY Observer*, sounds slightly dodgy, unserious. I've remained a Villager by living in a subsidized housing project that is a lonely outpost of the arts in the

Village, which is no longer an arts center. Today the spirit of bohemia has taken root in slightly rundown outposts like Long Beach, where they recognize me as one of their own.

It is odd that Long Beach poets don't take much interest in the Beats. Of course, there's rivalry with the San Francisco Bay Area. They're too young to remember the arrival on the scene of the Beats in the late-fifties like a cracking of the ice in spring. I also think that the bardic style of Ginsberg doesn't suit the sleazy everyday life of Southern California. Or my own daily struggle. We're deadbeat rather than beat.

Bukowski's movie *Barfly,* starring Mickey Rourke and Faye Dunaway, has the distinction of being one of the rare Hollywood movies ever written by a poet. Before him, James Agee adapted his Broadway play, "A Death in the Family," for a movie and James Dickey adapted "Deliverance" from his novel. Southwest poet Jimmy Santiago Baca wrote a movie about Chicano violence. But writing for the movies has always been considered beneath serious poets.

Gerald Locklin and Charles Stetler of Long Beach State University interviewed me in the late 60s for an essay and through them I got to know Ron Koertge who teaches in L.A. Locklin must be king of the small-press scene, with about a hundred and fifty chapbooks. Koertge, the most lyrical of the three, reflects a particularly L.A. mentality with poems about Superman, race tracks, porn shops, and a Joycean interest in panties. All three celebrate the seedy aspects of the male psyche.

"If Auden is the ideal schoolmaster, Cavafy the perfect guide to romantic depravity, and Bukowski the necessary buttkicker to bring us down to reality, Gerald Locklin is the lovable big brother everybody needs. Masterful but kind, he'd be generous in all things to us little kids, help us out of scrapes, stick up for us against phonies and bullies, and would never deny us our pleasures, whatever they are."

207

Quote for Ron Koertge: "These poems are fun the way they run off the tracks and yet make tremendous sense. No one will suffer reading his poetry. I can go even further: There is something holy about a poet who wants to give his readers nothing but pleasure."

ॐ

I was in London over Christmas,
when Gerald Locklin, who had been teaching in Wales,
stopped off on his way home to Long Beach
to give a poetry reading in a pub.
It was upstairs from the bar,
in a room with the scuffed look of a union hall,
or where a group of conspirators
might plan to throw a bomb—
perfect for Gerry.
I brought along a couple of friends
I was trying to interest in the Long Beach poetry scene,
but the reading wasn't publicized
and only about six of us were there.
While we waited in the rows of folding chairs
with glasses of beer in our hands,
we didn't know
that the promoter of the series
was at the bar below,
swilling it down for courage.
A pale youth, he finally appeared,
mumbled a few inarticulate words of introduction,
and sank into a chair.

Gerry announced his first poem,
"Every time I perform this piece,
I don't know why,
but something always happens…,"
when the sound of retching began.
It was the shy introducer, bent over,
with a hand to his mouth,

trying to staunch the flow.
As Gerry stood there
in his bemused, Olympian way,
holding his sheaf of poems,
the young poetry presenter,
still dribbling down his sweater,
staggered toward the exit at the rear,
pausing in the aisle to puke once more
in a great spray
over the stunned audience
and again at the door, where he let loose
a farewell flood.
Before resuming the reading,
Gerry commemorated the event by announcing,
in a voice full of awe at the human condition,
that it was the most unusual
response to his poetry
he ever got.

Gerry told me that the L.A. police cruising the streets were using the phrase "toothy lurker" from my poem "Sharks" over the patrol car radios to describe suspicious characters. One of the cops who hung out at The Forty-Niner, Gerry's favorite bar in Long Beach, heard him reading the poem, and started using the phrase, and then it got picked up by others in the department.

❧

From the Introduction to *A New Geography of Poets*

When my anthology, *A Geography of Poets,* came out in 1979, a top New York editor, who had the power to have it reviewed and didn't, declared to me point blank, "This is an anti-New York anthology." That of course was a negative interpretation of what it was trying to do, which was, by grouping poets according to where they lived, to show what was going on in the poetry scene in each part of the country, and for once, to give equal attention to each. For I had noticed in my years of touring the country doing readings at colleges that poets, good poets, were to be found, not just in a few cities and cultural centers, but everywhere in America. And everywhere they complained of neglect by the publishing/academic "establishment," which they located in the Northeast. So I conceived a geographical anthology that would act as a corrective to the situation, and present to the reader a fairer map of American poetry. The editor's reaction gives some indication of the power politics of poetry that the current *A New Geography of Poets* is trying to correct.

Without attacking New York City (which in many ways is the most liberal, intellectual city in the country, and frankly I wouldn't live anywhere else), many of us feel it unhealthy and undesirable that poetry should be dominated by the values of an elite, and what poetry we are likely to see filtered through a set of standards inappropriate to the interests of the rest of us. Especially when the liveliest developments in American poetry are for the most part ignored by the mandarins of Northeast academic criticism. At the opposite end of the country, the poets of Long Beach, for example, look to very different poetic models. They are closer to the young gay black poets I heard reading at a Pink Triangle Conference at CUNY Graduate Center, who live with AIDS, race discrimination, homophobia, and poverty.

In contrast to our mighty critics of poetry, it has always been my belief that poetry can be as interesting, if not necessarily as easy, to read as the newspaper, embody the idealism of the poetic impulse, and have a content that relates to real life, be it tragic, caustic, funny, or obscene.

At the time my first *Geography of Poets* was published, the liveliest alternative to the Northeast establishment, the opposite pole, as it were, was in the San Francisco Bay Area. For, beginning in the Fifties, San Francisco, with the explosion of Beat poetry, became a challenge to the hegemony of the East—anti-academic, political, exuberant. While Frank O'Hara and other poets of the New York School were surviving the gloomy McCarthyite days of witch hunts and artistic shutdown by attaching themselves to the emerging Abstract-Expressionist art scene, Allen Ginsberg, Lawrence Ferlinghetti, Gregory Corso, and Jack Kerouac left for San Francisco's more benign climate. The birth of Beat poetry there caused a sensation around the country and the world, and affected poetry profoundly. In fact, there was an explosion of poetry and a smashing of standards that split open for awhile the tight little island of the poetry world.

Today, with Beat poetry etched into history, the torch has been passed on to the Long Beach/Los Angeles nexus, which sees America very differently from a Beat Scene focusing on "righteous" issues. In a landscape the rest of the country fantasizes about, Southern Californian poets largely ignore the lotus-land mirage of orange groves, surfer beaches, and Disneyland, and find their material more often in the sleazier realities of life, commemorating the survival of humanity among the glitz, much as some of the poets of New York reflect the garbagey life of the Lower East Side, on the fringes of the glossy corporate city.

In contrast to the near-operatic poetry of the Beats, with its language of incantation, hyperbole, even preaching, the new poetry from the L.A./Long Beach area is laid back, more related to talk than song, invoking stand up comics, sassy comebacks, bar talk, and true confessions. Ideas are of less interest than telling the story of "what happened." As in the poetry of Charles Bukowski, cynicism is pervasive—love is often portrayed as alley-cats fighting, and financial problems are never far away. The bar and the mall are a common setting, as are ethnic neighborhoods, or the banal atmosphere of the Seven-Eleven. The feminism that the women poets seem to be expressing, ignoring the dogma of the movement, is the independence to take and talk sex as forthrightly as men.

The peculiar isolation of the Northeast literary establishment from the rest of the country is illustrated by a famous *New Yorker* cartoon, a map of America in which the towers of Manhattan loom large in the foreground, while across the Hudson River the rest of the country quickly dwindles away in the distance. As in the cartoon, the cultural establishment continues to hold the view that there is nothing much going on "out there" that is worth paying attention to. Whatever power games are

211

played in the halls of the cultural establishment, people might find the new vernacular poetry a pleasure to read and listen to, and as the barriers fall, admit poetry back to the racks of readable literature.

ह

From "The New Populist Poetry"
(published in *Poets and Writers*)

Nobody has quite been able to define it yet. Because it's easy to read, Steve Kowit, in his anthology *The Maverick Poets* called it Easy Poetry. For a long time, my friends in Long Beach, California, called it Long Beach poetry. Others call it Stand Up Poetry, used by Charles Webb as the title of his recent anthology. This refers partly to the fact that it has the flavor of the routines of stand up comics and partly to the title of my first book, *Stand Up, Friend, with Me*. I myself think of it as The Sassy Poetry of Southern California. No label quite works.

The poets of the New Populism, as they could be called, or Neo Pop for short, are usually from lower class backgrounds (as the founder of Pop Art, Andy Warhol, was), and they don't try to sound any different.

> you know
> I sat on the same barstool in Philadelphia for
> 5 years

begins "eddie and eve," by Charles Bukowski, who is the resident guru. Bukowski is a true *poète maudit* on the American literary scene. All but ignored in the Northeast, he has unaccountably become an international celebrity in his old age, a bestseller in several European countries. In this country, he is published by a small publisher, Black Sparrow Press, in Santa Rosa, California.

Many people drawn to poetry are disappointed when they try to read it. Something basic in what we expect from poetry is missing. Modern Poetry has mostly closed itself into an elegant, nearly-airless room where the uninitiated may not tread. The Beat revolution aside (a rebellion not to be dismissed), this is the

212

sterile world of High Literature, a kind of writing we considered fascist when I was young. That was a misnomer of course—fascism can as easily develop from populist illiteracy as from Jamesian strategies. And Neo Pop would not have been acceptable to the Left back then either, which demanded, along with working class subject matter, upbeat endings plus a morality veering toward puritanism. Neo Pop would have been classed as lumpen populism.

If you read the biggies of contemporary poetry, you'd think they weren't raised in America, with funnies, movies, radio, swing (in my generation), hadn't danced, didn't care about being unpopular. High class from the start, they felt superior to everything people around them (people like me!) were taken by. (John Ashbery is an exception: he's trashy *and* high class. Though I'm sure he never jitterbugged.)

There may be a naiveté to the new vernacular poetry, but the poets accept that they are products of America, growing up with popular music, movies, sports. If mass culture has debased literature, these poets don't know it. For instance, before getting his Ph.D. and teaching, Charles Stetler was a plumber, and still sounds like it sometimes:

> i love the Giffer,
> but it's really going to piss me off
> if i hear he's polishing off his ph.d.
> and plans to intercept my seminar in Joyce.
> — "A Man of Many Moves"

Neo Pop is related more to proletarian fiction, realism, naturalism, than to poetry, and like these genres often deals with bums, hoboes, sluts, low-lifers and marginals. The spirit is essentially goodhearted, but anti-dogmatic, and therefore sometimes seems to exhibit anti-feminist, anti-gay tendencies, even mysogyny. On the whole, this is not your left-wing, do-gooder populism, though it has the concerns of the common herd—sex, booze, making a buck, athletics, and television. It may ignore the high spiritual concerns of Stevens and Eliot, but its subject matter is extraordinarily varied, unashamedly reflecting the tawdriness, the philistinism of American daily life, taking place, characteristically, in the bars and shopping malls, on the freeways, at the racetracks, and in the porno shops, that the poets, as modern Americans, are perfectly at home in. Here is Ronald Koertge in a porn shop:

> My God, what a crowd this morning. As usual I am
> wearing a false mustache and my vagabond knave's
> disguise, but I am small change compared to the
>
> rest. At my left is the Superintendent of Schools
> in high drag, over there my former Sunday School
> teacher in a wino's get-up....
> —"In The Dirty Book Store"

and going to the track:

> Hollywood Park Race Track is thirty miles
> by tangled freeway from Los Alamitos Race
> Track, but lately I find myself at one of
> them all afternoon and at the other most
> of the night.
> —"Please"

Of course, your average person does not write, much less read, poetry, and in spite of the cult of the macho poet in the northwest, where poets work as lumberjacks and fishermen, poetry is as much a special activity as ever. Easy as the New Populist poetry is to read, the paradox behind its surface availability is expressed by Gerald Locklin, in his poem "Constituency Of Dunces":

> "your problem," she says, "is that the people
> to whom your work might appeal
> do not read poetry.
> in fact, most of those
> who might share your attitudes or viewpoint
>
> either don't or can't read at all."

214

There are poets writing out of this sensibility everywhere in the country now, even on the fringes in New York, where high culture rules. But New York poets tend toward a minimalist chic similar to the Bolinas school, which sees poetry as fragments assembled or scattered on the page, exemplified by notebook jottings or shopping lists published as poetry. The instinct behind this, when it is not loaded with academic freight like Olson and Pound, is honest: Don't make writing poetry such a big deal. Like Frank O'Hara writing poems on his lunch hour in his office in between telephone calls.

Vulgar, funny, dirty, sassy, Neo Pop doesn't aim particularly at tightness, though the expression is often succinct and precise. Nor is it obscure, it speaks right out, plainly and directly, in the language we use:

"Do you love me?" I asked.
"Love you? How could I love a toad?"

That made a lot of sense,
so I asked her, "How's about
if we just kind of sleep together?"
—"The Toad," by Gerald Locklin

Neo Pop is almost always written in free verse, in very casual forms, though the sense of form is strong. As in Beat Poetry, the shape of a poem is an organic development that carries itself through from beginning to end on the energy of the impulse, trusting what you have to say, rather than intensively worked over material, a hallmark of academic poetry. But Neo Pop doesn't have to be inflated to anything more than it is, or strain for an epiphany or insight—any momentary reaction will do. So this kind of poetry is not struggled for, sweated over—it is poetry viewed as a natural function, a natural expression. But it takes a kind of nerve to allow the poem to come out whole, skill to skirt the banal, and sophistication to make such a poem interesting and fun, even funny.

Here is Ronald Koertge's "Diary Cows":

> Got up early, waited for the farmer.
> He hooked us all to the machines as
> usual. Typical trip to the pasture,
> typical day grazing and ruminating.
> about 5:00 back to the machines. What
> relief! Listened to the radio
> during dinner. Lights out at 7:00.
> More tomorrow.

That a poem should say something interesting is one of the propelling ideas behind the New Populist poetry. This means that the language should not obscure what a poem means, but should tell the reader directly, even if it's a teenage fantasy:

> Robert Wagner lived in my closet
> the summer I was 14. Between movies,
> bored with Bel Aire and the Riviera, he
> lived amongst my skirts and sweaters
> and pedal pushers....
> —"Why Robert Wagner Married Natalie Wood,"
> by Joan Jobe Smith

Being obvious is no crime. And hopefully and God willing, it will have a couple of laughs in it, to make life less grim. For laughter is considered a proof of hitting the bull's-eye, a mark of freshness, originality, discovery.

The language of Neo Pop is not clean, respectable, academic, or usually poetic in the poetic sense.

> karl, my friend, caught the crabs.
> such a scrappy bunch, he admired,
> then grew accustomed to their ways.
> —"policy of the house," by Charles Stetler

It is a characteristic of much recent poetry, though not the kind published in *Poetry* magazine and other respectable journals, to talk about your sex life frankly, reveal sex secrets, use earthy and four-letter words, all of this unthinkable in the poetry world

216

before the Beats, and mighty rare since. Women have led the way in this unraveling of the prudish layers around modern poetry:

> We end up
> rolling around on the bed. He tells me
> he has only one ball.
> I feel. Yes, one ball
> but it's big. I show him
> my....
> —"Hungry," by Lisa Glatt

Does this poetry ignore the language function so many critics see as primary to poetry? Yes, it rejects the whole idea of poetic language, if by poetic you mean the fancy, self-conscious language promoted in writing workshops and by academic critics, the dense kind of language that poetry editors feel secure with. It rejects the dogma that you shouldn't be obvious in your poem, or it isn't poetry, that affectation is basic to poetry. It is also suspicious about grandiose effects, such as the Beats aim for, the rhetorical word riffs, the self-importance, the prophetic role—for this is the poetry of people who don't mind speaking plain, who insist on remaining unpretentious. They are talented, and use their talents, but it doesn't make them superior.

Taking a cue from my "old movie" poems in my book, *Variety Photoplays*, a number of the poets of Neo Pop started writing movie poems. Their exploitation of this genre is one of their most distinctive characteristics, and they have written wittily, often hilariously, about movies like "Shane" and "King Kong," created imaginary scripts, and tributes to movie stars. I'll end with a small roundup of excerpts, starting with a letter to Superman from Lois Lane:

> I know you think that things
> will always be the same: I'll rinse
> out your tights, kiss you goodbye
> at the window and every few weeks
> get kidnapped by some stellar goons.

217

But I'm not getting any younger
and you're not getting any older....
                —"Dear Superman," by Ronald Koertge

He rode into the valley with his wide brim hat way down almost
over his eyes but tall in the saddle
even though Alan Ladd was, I heard, only about five-five...
                —"Shane," by Charles Stetler

    as long as he could remember they'd been on
    his ass for playing with himself, his mother
    used to tell him, "herbert, for the last time
    keep your hands off that ugly thing...."
                —"The Snakeman of Alcatraz,"
                by Gerald Locklin

In my book, the biggest sin of poetry is to be boring, and, frankly, it's so often boring. Whatever else you can say about it, the New Populist poetry is not.

≈

From review of *Girl Soldier*, by Denise Duhamel; *Monsters and other Lovers*, by Lisa Glatt; *Blood Poisoning*, Poems, by Jeffery Conway

(in *Exquisite Corpse*)

When these three books by young poets came in the mail in the same week, I asked myself, "Are these the Brat Poets of the 90s?" Like the Brat Pack of the 80s they speak for a new generation, whose mentality is so different from mine. They have little historical awareness (of "us," do I mean?). Anne Sexton seems to be as far back as they go. Instead of Europe and Paris, they think that America and especially New York is the center of world culture. Instead of what we called politics, they have sexual and gender politics.

The thing that strikes me the most in this generation is the lack of political awareness, the lack of "social protest." These

218

young poets seem to accept society the way my friends never did. It is a post-Foucault universe, where capitalism and the military/industrial complex is considered too much of a bore to be the enemy. Or it's taken for granted it's the enemy, and it's understood that nothing can be done about. Subversiveness (they call it transgressiveness) alone might humanize it, or bring it down.

On the other hand, what is political about this generation is sex. Sex is political. Being a woman is political. Being gay is political.

Though extremely well-written, the poems in these three books, except for touches of surrealism, toss out most of our literary devices. They could hardly be called literary, yet are the most vivid poems imaginable, not in language, but in subject matter—lurid tales of sex lives lived to the hilt, spoken about with none of our artsy evasion, everything is there in entertaining detail. We had to use metaphor to deal with a lot of the embarrassing stuff. These poems discard obscurity, the benchmark of modern poetry, as just another label for the closet, or perhaps for irrelevant philosophizing.

Against the background of public prudery in my youth, I always found going as far as I could in writing about my intimate secrets to be a necessity and, though it was difficult to get those poems published, had the added fun of being considered scandalous, but in the atmosphere of public confession today it has become commonplace. What's special about it? There are far more lurid secrets than yours being proclaimed. This is a relief, because once subjects are no longer shocking, we can face them squarely.

One crucial element in the work of these three poets that makes them so different from my generation and is pure Brat Pack, is that they don't romanticize failure. They make me embarrassed to remember how we reveled in failure, in being "outsiders," in writhing in our beds of neurotic torment. But these three have no truck with that. They are conscious of a world out there where it is necessary to make it, and feel they have a right to. They are incredibly gifted, so I agree they ought to be right up there with the successful ones, and have no doubt they will be some day.

America has always been a scary place to me. Being different was dangerous. If you were different you were in danger. That's one reason I always wanted to get out of it. What about leaving the country for a while, I want to ask them, getting away from the rat race, as my generation called it? But to the young nowadays it doesn't seem so scary—is it that they wear blinders? It is more their place than it ever was for us. They are at home here. (The young don't see America from the outside as we did— as the enemy. They are completely part of it. But our souls are abroad as much as here, so we take a critical stance that they don't.)

Besides, with the economics of life today, they don't really have the choice of getting out. Leave the scene and you are forgotten.

Modern poetry has made a big issue of directing the reader to its language and style. What I like about Lisa Glatt's poems is that you can forget about them being poetry and read them just to find out about her life. When one of her legs was crushed in a childhood car accident, she was led to doubt that, in a world of perfect children, she could ever have sex with a man.

But in her case, there is also a mother, though not the Freudian Mother that my generation had. It is her mother's breast cancer operation that is the trauma (if our old-fashioned word applies) that throws her life even more out of whack and casts a lurid glow over her sex life, with an undercurrent of disgust with herself, especially with her lovers' fascination with her breasts.

Her exploration of these subjects alone makes the book a fascinating read, but her chronicle of the different men she dallies with also has a bracing honesty, that I ended up thinking, Why the fuck not?

Jeffery Conway's poetry, in its in-your-face style, is like an Act Up demonstration. But he has a double vision—through his present east village reality, where blood is the agent of death, the pre-AIDS Los Angeles of his youth keeps emerging. He gives a haunting portrait of his adolescence in California—remote parents, plenty of money, and the romance of evanescent punk rock groups. If drugs are not a factor, perhaps the incipient poet spaced out on rock music didn't need them, or they are so implicit in the stoned mentality, represented by a repeated fragment of a rock lyric, "Am I a photo? I can't remember," that they don't need even to be mentioned.

AIDS interrupts his romantic moments with a series of men, with blood often the flag of alarm—a cut from shaving, bleeding gums, or a sharp spike of grass—AIDS is simply there. Along with poison ivy and deer riddled with lyme disease on otherwise-glamorous Fire Island are the kaposi sarcoma lesions on the skin of the young.

His "confessional" title poem (quotation marks on purpose, since it is an old-fashioned genre now) relates the story about his older brother screwing him in the family swimming pool which has the earmarks of fantasy seen in much of the recovered-memory literature. All I can say is that if it happened, it's a pity it wasn't any fun.

From some of her earlier work, one might get the impression that Denise Duhamel is queen in a world of pink plastic. It was never true, since her poetry always trembled with compassion. But in this new collection the savage edge is exposed.

There's always been a strong anti-bimbo factor in her poems. She's written a lot of them from the mentality of Barbie Dolls. Underneath the satire, though, lies disappointment that the Barbie life is not possible, as the American dream is not possible. Her feminism, though, is the feminism of a woman who could get away with playing the bimbo game, even enjoy it, while observing the fakery of it, its limitations. So her understanding of the Barbie mentality is that she shares it, and is wise enough not to deny that—or rather sees that Barbie is one of the levels of our/her mentality.

Her poems on childhood are quite un-Barbie-like, as she fights with her sister, torments her mother, and suffers asthma attacks that make her a difficult date, the Date From Hell, in fact.

221

Or rather she fills in the Barbie outlines with real-life torments.

If her poems ever gave off a pink aura, a cute little girl ingenuousness, there is now a darker tone to them, the seriousness is showing more, meaning more is at stake. Perhaps her marriage to Nick Carbo, whose own recent book of poems *El Grupo McDonald's* looks unflinchingly at the Philippine society he grew up in, was the catalyst to this deepening of vision. There really are guerillas in the hills in countries like the Philippines, though guerillas of the left, rather than our own right-wing militias. This opening to the real world has radicalized her in a way that cuts through the confusion of the usual American political babble. Poems also go into the economics of surviving as a poet, which my old bohemian soul appreciates.

Like her contemporaries, Denise Duhamel also deals with her sex life in a forthright manner. We even learn about a lesbian lover, who is as difficult and disappointing as any of her own, Lisa Glatt's, or Jeffery Conway's, men. (In her husband's book there is a tender poem trying to explain to his devout Catholic mother that Denise is truly religious, but in her own way, confessing her sins via her poems to the world instead of the priest.) Hers is the poetry of a Barbie Doll who has cracked out of her painted plastic face and is dealing with the real world.

ॐ

LIVES OF THE POETS

> Robert Friend was so innocent
> that when he got his first hard-on
> he ran downstairs to the living room
> where the family was sitting around,
> listening to the radio
> and showed it to them:
> "Look!" he shouted, "It goes up, then it goes down.
> It goes up and down."
>
> They called him dummy
> and chased him from the room.

222

When I read the poems of Robert Friend, I always sense the relationship to my own poetry. He was the father who passed on to me the key, and his own poetry is the mother ground I started from. It is true that W. H. Auden and Constantine Cafavy were major influences on me almost from the beginning, but first there was Robert Friend.

LETTER TO ROBERT FRIEND

1

The news is bad, dear friend,
you tell me by telephone from Jerusalem,

but I'm only ten years behind you
so it won't be long before
I too have to face
the Big Issue.

As jaundice was the indicator of your current state,
who knows what that pain in my shoulder means?
I'd rather not look into it.
Medical treatments may make things better,
as with you now,
but often make them worse.
With your shaky voice over the phone
giving the alarming facts of your medical condition,
I thought you were calling to say goodbye,
but then you sounded completely yourself again,
and I saw that you were going to live
for as long as you have.

Just the same, I wonder if you have
anyone to talk to about death?
If I were there, we'd discuss it from A to Z
the way you examine a poem.
Assuming you go first,
how you go is of vital interest to me,

your student in all things,
starting with Poetry.

2

You became one of the most important people in my life,
when we met on the ship to France in 1948.
A group gathered around you,
young men drawn by the magic
of your pedagogical, and pedophilic, interest.
When I showed you my poems,
you suggested, with no mercy, writing short stories.
You made it clear that poetry
was a life and death matter—for life.
But after we spent many hours sitting in cafés
in Paris and Perpignan and Paris again,
talking poetry and studying
the Oscar Williams anthology of modern verse
like the Bible,
I turned out some lines you approved of,
or maybe it was just my intensity, my desperation,
the hopelessness of doing anything else with my life—
and I became your disciple.

Whether or not poetry can be taught,
I know that you transmitted it,
revealed it,
by opening yourself to me
in an age-old master/pupil process.
You must have sensed in me a soul
hungry for The Knowledge
and capable of using it.
That meant showing me what you were working on
and letting me examine it, question it,
explore what you did
and see how a poem grew,
draft after draft,
in your case, hundreds of drafts.

224

The means became mine, and my poetry
to this day
reflects yours.

Of course, mine became completely mine,
and almost immediately I started sounding like me,
even before I went to Greece and discovered Cavafy.
So there were influences beyond yours,
but you laid down the matrix,
the mother field that nurtures me.

3

Even Christian Scientists die,
but, leaving Christ out of it,
I'd say their principle is correct:
There is no error in the universe,
harsh as that sounds.
And the body, no matter how far gone,
heals itself.
The difficult part is to remove yourself
and let it.

There is
no error
in the universe,
and the body
is self-healing
and self-correcting.
This is my night-time prayer
and is all that I can offer you.
It might at least alleviate
the panic in the night.
It helps me.

Still, everyone's situation is different
and maybe you will find your own words
for the healing principle,
to invoke the healing process.

I will be so sorry to see you die,
if indeed you die before me,
which is not at all certain—
we're both old guys who have lived our lives.
None of us knows how long it will be now,
though it will not be too far in the future
for either of us.

But how to accept the indignities
of the deteriorating body
with a calm and holy spirit?

Dear Robert, teacher, friend,
please stay around as long as you can,
and at the end, teach me,
as you have taught me so much already,
to welcome death as a Friend.

If Yehuda Amichai were not Israel's leading poet, Robert Friend would be its grand old man of poetry—in English.

January 13, 1998. Robert Friend's death. It feels like a star has fallen from the sky. Too late to dedicate a book to him. How could I never have done it before? "For Robert Friend, too late."

I started writing more than fifty years ago, and it feels strange that I should still be at it. It's exhilarating, even working with a deteriorating instrument. Cavafy sums it up best:

An old man in tears before the Muse:
In my whole life, he complains,
I have only written a few
slim books of poetry,
and gotten little attention for them.
I even see it in your pitiless eyes:
Why didn't I do more?

Perhaps they *were* too slim, too few.
But how to explain....

226

If I didn't try hard enough,
I don't even know why,
but always, other things
seemed to be more important.
Tell me, have I wasted my life,
as well as my talents?

Thus replies the statue:
Wipe your tears, old man.
You have taken a step
on the difficult ladder of poetry,
and even getting to the first rung
is an accomplishment the gods all praise.
Feel good about that, with my blessings,
for on this path
there is no failure.

LIVES OF THE POETS

I heard that on his deathbed, Howard Moss had a visit from a young lover. "Pull down your pants," Howard told him, "and show me your ass."

Daniel did,
and satisfied,
Howard died,

The trouble with poetry about old age is that nobody wants to hear about it. In London, recently, Diana Athill gave me cautionary advice, telling me about Roy Campbell's last books, one unbearable poem after another a groan of misery. This seems impossible to avoid, though. I can't help cataloging the deaths, the horrors.

It sometimes seems that there's little connection between me and the "poetry world" anymore. Whatever I've done is past, the balloon of my success has deflated. Anyway, I was always uncomfortable with success, and did my best to derail it. I was more comfortable with failure.

My reputation is like a balloon:
The string snapped and it floated away.

I can only hope to go on writing poems until the end, with the computer helping the enfeebling powers of old age.

I'm fading,
like an opera singer whose voice is gone,
but continues to do what she can,
little ballads and folks songs.

Critics say
she never had a spectacular voice
but it was warm and golden,
and held heartbreak.

La Passionaria, addressing the defeated Republicans in Barcelona in 1938 at the end of the Spanish Civil War:

"You can go proudly.
You are history.
You are legend."

Poetry,
a path where my least effort
has been a thousandfold returned.

᠈ᴗ

Printed June 1998 in Santa Barbara
& Ann Arbor for the Black Sparrow Press by
Mackintosh Typography & Edwards Brothers Inc.
Text set in Baskerville by Words Worth.
Design by Barbara Martin.
This first edition is published in paper wrappers;
there are 250 hardcover trade copies;
100 hardcover copies have been numbered & signed
by the author; & 20 copies handbound in boards
by Earle Gray are lettered A–T
& signed by the poet.

EDWARD FIELD was born June 7, 1924 in Brooklyn, New York, and grew up on Long Island, where he played cello in the Field Family Trio over radio station WGBB. During World War II he flew 25 missions over Europe. After a short time at New York University on the GI Bill, he returned to Europe where he began writing seriously—the details can be found in the poem "Bio"—and his poems started appearing in literary magazines, from *Botteghe Oscure, Evergreen Review,* and *The New York Review of Books* to *Wormwood Review, Exquisite Corpse,* and *American Poetry Review.* His first book, *Stand Up, Friend, with Me,* won the Lamont Award in 1962, followed by a Guggenheim Fellowship, the Prix de Rome, the Shelley Memorial Award, and a Lambda Award for his last book, *Counting Myself Lucky: Selected Poems, 1963–1992.* He has given readings at the Library of Congress and at universities all over the country, and has taught workshops at the Poetry Center–YMHA, Sarah Lawrence and other colleges.

Besides collections of poetry, which include an illustrated book of his movie poems, he has edited anthologies of modern pooetry and wrote the narration for the documentary film, *To Be Alive,* which won an Academy Award. He collaborates on fiction with Neil Derrick, under the pseudonym of Bruce Elliot. He is also the editor of *The Alfred Chester Newsletter,* and has prepared several volumes of Chester's work for Black Sparrow Press. He lives in New York, but spends as much time as he can in foreign places.